FERRARI
TUNING TIPS
AND
MAINTENANCE TECHNIQUES

by

GERALD L. ROUSH

and

JOHN R. APEN

NOTE FROM THE PUBLISHER

We are proud to have been able to work with Gerald Roush and John Apen on republishing this important work. Out-of-print and largely unavailable for years, Ferrari Tuning Tips & Maintenance Techniques was originally published by Jim Riff as Ferrari Tuning Tips & Techniques. Following two highly successful editions Gerald Roush and John Apen expanded and revised the work, which subsequently went through three printings from 1975 to 1977. Even though it has been nearly 25 years since its last revision, Ferrari Tuning Tips & Maintenance Techniques still contains essential information for the Ferrari enthusiast and mechanic.

It is our hope that this book serves your informational needs for years to come. Many more titles of interest to the classic automobile enthusiast are available via our website at www.VelocePress.com.

Stephen Glenn
Publisher
VelocePress

This work may not be reproduced or transmitted in any form or format without the express written consent of the Publisher.

© 2001 Gerald L. Roush and John R. Apen

Published by TheValueGuide, Inc., Reno, NV 89509

ISBN Number 1-58850-012-8

DISCLAIMER

This book is presented as a historical reference work and has not been updated since its last publication in April, 1977. The names and addresses contained within have probably long since changed and some of the techniques have been superseded by more modern or environmentally friendly approaches. As with all complicated machinery we recommend consultation with and proper training by a qualified mechanic before attempting any repair detailed herein. While relatively commonplace and inexpensive at the time of writing, many of the machines treated within are now highly sought-after collectibles of considerable value. Please make sure that you are qualified before you "insert your gold plated screwdriver into the works."

INTRODUCTION

(The original introduction - April, 1977 edition)

All Ferraristi owe a tremendous debt to Jim Riff, especially those who would find it impossible to own an example of the marque if they had to depend on hiring someone to do their routine service and maintenance. Several years ago, when Jim first came out with the original version of Ferrari Tuning Tips and Techniques, there was nothing to guide the Ferrari owner who wanted to do some of his own service through the intricacies of the more routine service procedusres.

For the past couple of years FAF Motorcars has been the sole distributor of Jim's manual. And, for some time we have been aware that an updated, expanded and revised version was necessary. When our stock of the manual ran out in the Summer of 1975, we decided it was time to go ahead and make the revisions. The labor and headache involved in creating this new edition have increased our admiration of Jim Riff and his pioneer effort. We had Jim's manual to use as a starting point. Jim didn't have any such advantage.

The recommendations and suggestions contained herein have been collected and compiled from many sources. Some of them we have personally checked out, while others have been accepted on the word of an "authority." We therefore do not express and are not responsible for any claims implied or expressed herein. We have attempted to give credit where credit was due to others for their information, but found that we had many unidentified notes in our files. For those of you whom we should have recognized but didn't, please accept our apologies.

Anyone seriously interested in pursuing the practice of self servicing their Ferrari should avail themselves of as much of the factory literature - - owners manuals, workshop manuals, spare parts catalogs, etc. - - as is available for their car. We assume that you are already familiar with FAF Motorcars' catalog, the Ferrari Owners Survival Manual, although we have attempted to refrain from plugging the services of FAF too much in this manual. Many of the items mentioned herein are available from FAF even if we don't say so in the text.

While attempting to improve on the earlier editions - - for instance you will find the tips grouped together by subject in much the same manner as the factory manuals - - we do not claim this manual is complete or perfect. We are sure we have left something out, and that something we have put in is wrong. But, as Jim Riff pointed out in the earlier editions, there are many tips available to the Ferrari owner; go forth and seek them out. They are there. And when you find them, let us know about them. We invite your comments and suggestions, and welcome additional tips. We are already thinking about the next edition.

Gerald L. Roush

John R. Apen

Table of Contents

SECTION 1 - SPECIFICATIONS 7

SECTION II - ENGINE PART A - BASIC ENGINE 23

SECTION II - ENGINE PART B - ENGINE FUEL AND CARBURETION SYSTEM 39

SECTION II - ENGINE PART C - ENGINE IGNITION SYSTEM 55

SECTION II - ENGINE PART D - ENGINE COOLING SYSTEM 65

SECTION II - ENGINE PART E - ENGINE LUBRICATION SYSTEM 73

SECTION II - ENGINE PART F - ENGINE EXHAUST SYSTEM 77

SECTION III - CLUTCH AND TRANSMISSION 81

SECTION IV – DRIVE SHAFT 91

SECTION V – DIFFERENTIAL AND REAR AXLE 93

SECTION VI - REAR SUSPENSION 95

SECTION VII - FRONT SUSPENSION 95

SECTION VIII - SHOCK ABSORBERS 99

SECTION IX - STEERING 103

SECTION X - BRAKES 105

SECTION XI - WHEELS AND TIRES 117

SECTION XII - ELECTRICAL SYSTEM 121

SECTION XIII - BODYWORK AND TRIM 133

SECTION XIV - MISCELLANEOUS 143

APPENDIX A - WEBER CARBURETOR DIAGRAMS 153

SECTION 1 - SPECIFICATIONS

Ferraris have always been individualistic automobiles, a characteristic, which adds to their mystique, but which also, makes tabulating their specifications difficult. With the earlier types, each example was usually unique in some aspect, and even after the advent of "mass production" with the 250 GT, specification changes were made as needed, expediency, improvement, or customer's preference dictated. Within each range there are many variations – six carburetor set-ups on normally three carburetor engineers, racing cams in touring engines, alloy bodied examples of steel bodied types, etc.

The following specification tables deal only with the basic physical specifications, and cover only the more popular types since the advent of the 250 GT. Additional specifications will be found in the relevant sections. Where possible, only official factory publications have been used as sources. In many instances, even these differ. An example of this is with the 250 GT Berlinetta Lusso. Two different factory brochures give different engine power and torque specifications, while a factory technical service bulletin refers to a "Series 1" and a "Series 2" Lusso.

Finally, we are aware that there are discrepancies in conversion from Metric to English units. We give you what the factory published, with only an occasional correction. And don't forget that the factory figures for capacities and consumption are usually computed using Imperial measurements, not United States.

SPECIFICATIONS – 250 GT PININFARINA COUPE CHASSIS TYPE 508D ENGINE TYPE 128D

PRINCIPAL DATA

Wheelbase	2600 mm	102.4 in
Front tread (at static load)	1354 mm	53.3 in
Rear tread (at static load)	1349 mm	53.1 in
Turning circle	10.0 m	33 ft
Body work		Closed
Number of seats		Two (2)

DIMENSIONS

Overall length (including bumpers)	4395 mm	173.0 in
Overall width	1650 mm	65.0 in
Overall height (unladen)	1400 mm	55.0 in
Minimum ground clearance (laden)	170 mm	6.7 in

WEIGHT

Curb weight (with water, oil and spare tire)	1225 kg	2700 lb
Overall weight (full load plus two persons)	1520 kg	3350 lb
Fuel consumption per 100 km	18 lt	14 mpg
Cruising range (normal driving w/normal load)	600 km	375 mls

ENGINE

Number and arrangement of cylinders		V-12 60°
Bore and stroke	73x58.8 mm	2.87x2.28 in
Cubic displacement	2953.211 cc	180.5 ci
Compression ratio		8.5 to 1
Maximum horsepower		240
Engine speed at maximum power		7000 rpm
Maximum torque	25 kgm	181 ft lb
Engine speed at maximum torque		5000 rpm
Specific power, horsepower/litre		80
Italian fiscal rating		38.6 H

Source:
<u>Directions for Use and Upkeep of the Ferrari 250 Granturismo</u>, page 2.
<u>Road & Track</u>, June 1960, page 35.

SPECIFICATIONS – 250 GTE 2+2 CHASSIS TYPE 508E ENGINE TYPE 128E OR 128R

PRINCIPAL DATA

Wheelbase	2600 mm	8 ft 6 in
Front tread (at static load)	1395 mm	4 ft 7 in
Rear tread (at static load)	1387 mm	4 ft 6 in
Turning circle	12.2 m	40 ft 1 in
Body work		Closed
Number of seats		Four (2+2)

DIMENSIONS

Overall length (including bumpers)	4700 mm	15 ft 5 in
Overall width	1710 mm	5 ft 7 in
Overall height (unladen)	1340 mm	4 ft 5 in
Minimum ground clearance	145 mm	5 in

WEIGHT

Curb weight (with water, oil and spare tire)	1310 kg	2890 lb
Overall weight (full load plus four persons)	1695 kg	3740 lb
Fuel consumption per 100 km	16 lt	14 mpg
Cruising range (normal driving w/normal load)	500 km	310 mls

ENGINE

Number and arrangement of cylinders	V-12	60°
Bore and stroke	73x58.8 mm	2.87x2.28 in
Cubic displacement	2953.211 cc	180.5 ci
Compression ratio		9.2 to 1
Maximum horsepower		235
Engine speed at maximum power		7000 rpm
Maximum torque	25 kgm	181 ft lb
Engine speed at maximum torque		5000 rpm
Specific power, horsepower/litre		78
Italian fiscal rating		38.6 HP

Source:
250 GT/E Coupe Pininfarina 2+2 Operating, Maintenance and Service Handbook, page 5.

SPECIFICATIONS – 250 GT BERLINETTA LUSSO CHASSIS TYPE 539 ENGINE TYPE 168

PRINCIPAL DATA

Wheelbase	2400 mm	94.4 in
Front tread (at static load)	1395 mm	55.0 in
Rear tread (at static load)	1387 mm	54.8 in
Turning circle	12.0 m	39.3 ft
Body work		Closed
Number of seats		Two (2)

DIMENSIONS

Overall length (including bumpers)	4400 mm	173.5 in
Overall width	1650 mm	65.0 in
Overall height (unladen)	1290 mm	50.8 in
Minimum ground clearance (laden)	120 mm	4.7 in
Overhang from front axle	840 mm	33.0 in
Overhang from rear axle	1175 mm	46.2 in

WEIGHT

Dry weight	1020 kg	2250 lb
Curb weight (with water, oil and spare tire)	1360 kg	2995 lb
Overall weight (full load plus one person)	1470 kg	3250 lb
Weight on front axle	705 kg	1560 lb
Weight on rear axle	765 kg	1690 lb
Fuel consumption per 100 km	16/18 lt	12/14 mpg
Cruising range (normal driving w/normal load)	650 km	400 mls

ENGINE

Number and arrangement of cylinders		V-12 60°
Bore and stroke	73x58.8 mm	2.87x2.28 in
Cubic displacement	2953.211 cc	180.5 ci
Compression ratio		9.2 to 1
Maximum horsepower		240 to 290
Engine speed at maximum power		7000 or 7500 rpm
Maximum torque	25 or 30 kgm	181 or 218 ft lb
Engine speed at maximum torque		5000 or 5500 rpm
Specific power, horsepower/litre		80 or 97
Italian fiscal rating		38.6 HP

Source:
Sales brochures published by Ferrari.
<u>Road & Track</u>, June 1969, page 37.

SPECIFICATIONS – 275 GTB/GTS CHASSIS TYPE 563 ENGINE TYPE 213

PRINCIPAL DATA	275 GTB	275 GTS
Wheelbase	2400 mm	2400 mm
Front tread (at static load)	1377 mm	1377 mm
Rear tread (at static load)	1393 mm	1393 mm
Turning circle	14.07 m	14.07 m
Body work	Closed	Open
Number of seats	2	2 + 1

DIMENSIONS

	275 GTB	275 GTS
Overall length (including bumpers)	4325 mm	4370 mm
Overall width	1725 mm	1680 mm
Overall height (unladen)	1245 mm	1310 mm
Minimum ground clearance (laden)	120 mm	120 mm
Overhang from front axle	840 mm	860 mm
Overhang from rear axle	1085 mm	1110 mm

WEIGHT

	275 GTB	275 GTS
Curb weight (with water, oil and spare tire)	1100 kg	1150 kg
Overall weight (full load plus two persons)	1455 kg	1506 lb
Weight on front axle	649 kg	723 kg
Weight on rear axle	806 kg	783 kg
Fuel consumption per 100 km	18/20 lt	18/20 lt
Cruising range (normal driving w/normal load)	495 km	450 km

ENGINE

	275 GTB	275 GTS
Number and arrangement of cylinders	V-12 60°	V-12 60°
Bore and stroke (mm)	77x58.8	77x58.8
Cubic displacement (cc)	3285.722	3285.722
Compression ratio	9.2 to 1	9.2 to 1
Maximum horsepower	280	260
Engine speed at maximum power	7600 rpm	7000 rpm
Maximum torque (kgm)	30	28
Engine speed at maximum torque	5500 rpm	5000 rpm
Specific power, horsepower/litre	85	80
Italian fiscal rating	41.4	41.4

Source:
<u>Spyder 275 GTS Berlinetta 275 GTB Assembly Data and Overhaul Instructions</u>, page 3.

SPECIFICATIONS – 330 GT 2+2 CHASSIS TYPE 571 ENGINE TYPE 209

PRINCIPAL DATA

Wheelbase	2650 mm	8 ft 8 5/16 in
Front tread (at static load)	1397 mm	4 ft 6 5/8 in
Rear tread (at static load)	1389 mm	4 ft 6 9/16 in
Turning circle	13.78 m	4 ft 6 9/16 in
Body work		Closed
Number of seats		Four (2+2)

DIMENSIONS

Overall length (including bumpers)	4840 mm	15 ft 10 ½ in
Overall width	1715 mm	5 ft 7 ½ in
Overall height (unladen)	1360 mm	4 ft 5 ½ in
Minimum ground clearance	120 mm	4 ¾ in
Overhang from front axle	880 mm	2 ft 10 5/8 in
Overhang from rear axle	1310 mm	4 ft 3 9/16 in

WEIGHT

Curb weight (with water, oil and spare tire)	1380 kg	3042 lb
Overall weight (full load plus four persons)	1762 kg	3884 lb
Weight on front axle	804 kg	1772 lb
Weight on rear axle	958 kg	2112 lb
Fuel consumption per 100 km	18/20 lt	12 mpg
Cruising range (normal driving w/normal load)	480 km	300 mls

ENGINE

Number and arrangement of cylinders		V-12 60°
Bore and stroke	77x71 mm	3.03x2.80 in
Cubic displacement	3976 cc	242 ci
Compression ratio		8.8 to 1
Maximum horsepower		300
Engine speed at maximum power		6600 rpm
Maximum torque	32.5 kgm	236 ft lb
Engine speed at maximum torque		5500 rpm
Specific power, horsepower/litre		75
Italian fiscal rating		46.8 HP

Source:
330 GT Operating, Maintenance and Service Handbook, page 7.

SPECIFICATIONS – 330 GTC CHASSIS TYPE 592 ENGINE TYPE 209

PRINCIPAL DATA

Wheelbase	2400 mm	94.5 in
Front tread (at static load)	1401 mm	55.2 in
Rear tread (at static load)	1417 mm	55.7 in
Turning circle	13.95 m	45.8 ft
Body work	Closed	
Number of seats	Two (2)	

DIMENSIONS

Overall length (including bumpers)	4470 mm	14.8 ft
Overall width	1665 mm	65.5 in
Overall height (unladen)	1282 mm	50.5 in
Minimum ground clearance	120 mm	4.7. in
Overhang from front axle	940 mm	37.0 in
Overhang from rear axle	1130 mm	44.5 in

WEIGHT

Curb weight (with water, oil and spare tire)	1300 kg	2860 lb
Overall weight (full load plus four persons)	1595 kg	3520 lb
Weight on front axle	750 kg	1655 lb
Weight on rear axle	845 kg	1865 lb
Fuel consumption per 100 km	18/20 lt	12 mpg
Cruising range (normal driving w/normal load)	450 km	280 mls

ENGINE

Number and arrangement of cylinders	V-12	60°
Bore and stroke	77x71 mm	3.03x2.80 in
Cubic displacement	3976 cc	242 ci
Compression ratio	8.8 to 1	
Maximum horsepower	300	
Engine speed at maximum power	6600 rpm	
Maximum torque	32.5 kgm	236 ft lb
Engine speed at maximum torque	5500 rpm	
Specific power, horsepower/litre	75	
Italian fiscal rating	46.8 HP	

Source:
Coupe 330 GTC Dati di Montaggio e Istruzioni per le Revisioni, page 1.
330 GTC Operating, Maintenance and Service Handbook, page 9.

SPECIFICATIONS – 365 GT 2+2 CHASSIS TYPE 591 ENGINE TYPE 245

PRINCIPAL DATA

Wheelbase	2650 mm	104 in
Front tread (at static load)	1438 mm	56.5 in
Rear tread (at static load)	1468 mm	58 in
Turning circle	13.60 m	44.6 ft
Body work		Closed
Number of seats		Four (2+2)

DIMENSIONS

Overall length (including bumpers)	4974 mm	195 in
Overall width	1786 mm	70 in
Overall height (unladen)	1345 mm	53 in
Minimum ground clearance	130 mm	5 in
Overhang from front axle	1021 mm	40.2 in
Overhang from rear axle	1310 mm	51.6 in

WEIGHT

Curb weight (with water, oil and spare tire)	1823 kg	4020 lb
Overall weight (full load plus four persons)	2175 kg	4800 lb
Fuel consumption per 100 km	20/22 lt	12/14 mpg
Cruising range (normal driving w/normal load)	450 km	290 mls

ENGINE

Number and arrangement of cylinders	V-12	60°
Bore and stroke	81x71 mm	3.19x2.79 in
Cubic displacement	4290 cc	268 ci
Compression ratio		8.8 to 1
Maximum horsepower		320
Engine speed at maximum power		6600 rpm
Maximum torque	42.5 kgm	308 ft lb
Engine speed at maximum torque		5000 rpm
Italian fiscal rating		50.2 HP

Source:
<u>365 GT 2+2 Operating, Maintenance and Service Handbook</u>, pages 9-10.
<u>Road & Track, November 1969</u>, page 43.

SPECIFICATIONS – 365 GTB/4 CHASSIS TYPE 605 ENGINE TYPE 251

PRINCIPAL DATA

Wheelbase	2400 mm	7 ft 11 in
Front tread (at static load)	1440 mm	4 ft 8 in
Rear tread (at static load)	1453 mm	4 ft 9 in
Turning circle	13 m	43 ft 0 in
Body work		Closed
Number of seats		Two (2)

DIMENSIONS

Overall length (including bumpers)	4425 mm	14 ft 6 in
Overall width	1760 mm	5 ft 10 in
Overall height (unladen)	1245 mm	4 ft 1 in
Minimum ground clearance	120 mm	4.7 in

WEIGHT

Dry weight	1280 kg	2820 lb
Overall weight (full load plus two persons)	1798 kg	3960 lb
Weight on front axle	848 kg	1870 lb
Weight on rear axle	950 kg	2090 lb
Fuel consumption per 100 km	20/23 lt	12/14 mpg
Cruising range (normal driving w/normal load)	450 km	280 mls

ENGINE

Number and arrangement of cylinders	V-12	60°
Bore and stroke	81x71 mm	3.19x2.79 in
Cubic displacement	4390 cc	268 ci
Compression ratio		8.8 to 1
Maximum horsepower		352 bhp (S.A.E. net)
Engine speed at maximum power		7500 rpm
Maximum torque	44 kgm	318 ft lb
Engine speed at maximum torque		5500 rpm
Italian fiscal rating		50.2 HP

Source:
Berlinetta 365 GTB4 Dati di Montaggio e Istruzioni per le Revisioni, page 7.
365 GTB/4 Operating Maintenance and Service Handbook, page 7.

SPECIFICATIONS – 365 GTC/4 CHASSIS TYPE 616 ENGINE TYPE 260 F 101 AC 000

PRINCIPAL DATA

Wheelbase	2500 mm	98.4 in
Front tread (at static load)	1480 mm	58.3 in
Rear tread (at static load)	1480 mm	58.3 in
Turning circle	13 m	43 ft
Body work		Closed
Number of seats		2+2

DIMENSIONS

Overall length (including bumpers)	4550 mm	177.2 in
Overall width	1780 mm	70.0 in
Overall height (unladen)	1270 mm	50.0 in
Minimum ground clearance (laden)	120 mm	4.7 in

WEIGHT

Curb weight (with oil, fuel, and spare wheel Tool kit and accessories)	1730 kg	3820 lb

ENGINE

Number and arrangement of cylinders		V-12 60°
Bore and stroke	81x71 mm	3.19x2.79 in
Cubic displacement	4390 cc	268 ci
Compression ratio		8.8 to 1
Maximum horsepower		320 bhp (S.A.E. net)
Engine speed at maximum power		6200 rpm
Maximum torque	44 kgm	318 ft lb
Engine speed at maximum torque		4000 rpm
Italian fiscal rating		50.2 HP

Source:
365 GTC/4 Operating, Maintenance and Service Handbook, pages 81, 88 and 90.

SPECIFICATIONS – DINO 246 GT CHASSIS TYPE 246 GT ENGINE TYPE 135 CS

PRINCIPAL DATA

Wheelbase	2340 mm	92.3 in
Front tread (at static load)	1425 mm	56 in
Rear tread (at static load)	1430 mm	56.3 in
Turning circle	11.4 m	37.5 ft
Body work	Closed	
Number of seats	Two (2)	

DIMENSIONS

Overall length (including bumpers)	4235 mm	166.7 in
Overall width	1700 mm	67.2 in
Overall height (unladen)	1135 mm	44.6 in

WEIGHT

Dry weight	1080 kg	2380 lb
Fuel consumption per 100 km	14/15 lt	18/20 mpg
Cruising range (normal driving w/normal load)	350 km	215 mls

ENGINE

Number and arrangement of cylinders	V-6	65°
Bore and stroke	92.5x60 mm	3.64x2.36 in
Cubic displacement	2418 cc	148.1 ci
Compression ratio	9.0 to 1	
Maximum horsepower	195	
Engine speed at maximum power	7600 rpm	
Maximum torque	23 kgm	165.5 ft lb
Engine speed at maximum torque	5500 rpm	
Italian fiscal rating	26.7 HP	

Source:
<u>Dino 246 GT Operating, Maintenance and Service Handbook</u>, pages 11-12.

SPECIFICATIONS: FUEL, LUBRICANT AND COOLANT CAPACITIES

NOTE: All capacities listed are in litres

	250 GTE 2+2	250 GT LUSSO	275 GTS	275 GTB	330 GT 2+2
FUEL TANK	90	114	86	94	90
FUEL RESERVE			14/16	14/16	15/21
RADIATOR			8.2	8.2	7
COOLING SYSTEM, TOTAL	11	11	12	12	14
OIL, SUMP & FILTERS	9	9	10	10	10
GEARBOX	3.5	3.25	4.5	4.5	Mk 1 3.25 Mk 2 5.0
DIFFERENTIAL	2.5	Mk 1 1.25 Mk 2 2.50			Mk 1 1.80 Mk 2 2.50
OVERDRIVE	1.0	n/a	n/a	n/a	Mk 1 1.0 Mk 2 n/a
STEERING BOX	0.4	0.4	0.4	0.4	0.4
BRAKING SYSTEM			0.81	0.81	0.81
CLUTCH SYSTEM			0.25	0.25	
FRONT SHOCK ABSORBERS			0.22	0.22	0.32
REAR SHOCK ABSORBERS			0.30	0.30	0.35
WINDSHIELD WASHER			0.5	0.5	0.5

SPECIFICATIONS: FUEL, LUBRICANT AND COOLANT CAPACITIES (Continued)

NOTE: All capacities listed are in litres

	330 GTC	365 GT 2+2	365 GTB/4	365 GTC/4	DINO 246 GT
FUEL TANK	90	112	128	105	70
FUEL RESERVE	14/16	14/16	18/20	14/16	12/14
RADIATOR	8.9	10.4		10.4	
COOLING SYSTEM, TOTAL	14	14	17.5	13	17
OIL, SUMP & FILTERS	10	10	16	16	7
OIL COOLER	n/a	0.75	n/a	0.75	n/a
GEARBOX	4.5	5	4.5	5	4.0
DIFFERENTIAL		2.5		2.5	
STEERING BOX	0.4	1.0	0.4	1.0	0.2
BRAKING SYSTEM	0.81	0.81	1.0	0.58	0.58
FRONT SHOCK ABSORBERS	0.22	0.35	0.19	0.35	0.19
REAR SHOCK ABSORBERS	0.30	0.31	0.26	0.31	0.26
WINDSHIELD WASHER	1.0	1.0	1.0	1.0	1.0

SPECIFICATIONS: FUEL, LUBRICANT AND COOLANT RECOMMENDATIONS

FUEL: ALL TYPES
Premium Gasoline, 98/100 Octane Rating

COOLANT: ALL TYPES
Pure Water or Water/Antifreeze Mixture

ENGINE OIL: TYPES 250 GTE 2_2, 275 GTS/GTB, 330 GT 2+2 AND 330 GTC
Above +15°C (+60°F) Shell X-100 SAE 40 or Multigrade 20W/40
From -5°C to +15°C   Shell X-100 SAE 30 or Multigrade 20W/40
Below -5°C (+20°F)   Shell X-100 SAE 20 or Multigrade 10W/30

ENGINE OIL: TYPE 365 CT 2+2
All Seasons   Shell Super Motor Oil 100
Or, as an alternative
Above 0°C (+32°F)   Shell X-100 SAE 40
Below 0°C (+32°F)   Shell X-100 SAE 30

ENGINE OIL: TYPES 365 GTB/4 and 365 GTC/4
Above -15° (+5°F)   Shell Super Motor Oil
Or, as an alternative
Above +15°C (+60°F) Shell X-100 SAE 40
From -5°C to +15°C   Shell X-100 SAE 30
Below -°C (+20°F)   Shell X-100 10W/30

ENGINE OIL: TYPE DINO 246 GT
For Normal Use   Shell Super Motor Oil 100
Below -15°C (+5°F)   Shell Super Motor Oil or Shell X-100 10W/30

GEARBOX LUBRICANT: TYPES 250 GTE 2+2, 330 GT 2+2 and 365 GT 2+2
Shell Spirax EP 90 or Shell Spirax HD 90

GEARBOX LUBRICANT: TYPE 365 GTC/4
Shell Spirax EP 80 or Shell Spirax HD 90

DIFFERENTIAL LUBRICANT: TYPES 250 GTE 2+2 and 330 GT 2+2
Shell Dentax 350, Shell Spirax EP 250, or Shell Spirax EP 140

DIFFERENTIAL LUBRICANT: TYPE 365 GT 2+2
Shell S 4796 A or Shell S 1747 A

DIFFERENTIAL LUBRICANT: TYPES 365 GTC/4
Shell Spirax HD 90

TRANSAXLE LUBRICANT: TYPES 275 GTS/GTB, 330 GTC AND 365 GTB/4
   Shell S 6721 A or Shell S 1747 A

TRANSAXLE LUBRICANT: TYPE DINO 246 GT
   Shell Spirax EP 80 or Shell Spirax HD 90

OVERDRIVE LUBRICANT: TYPES 250 GTE 2+2 and 330 GT 2+2
   Shell Spirax EP 90

STEERING BOX LUBRICANT: TYPES 250 GTE 2+2, 275 GTS/GTB, 330 GT 2+2, 330 GTC, and 365 GTB/4
   Shell Dentax EP 140 or Shell Spirax EP 140

STEERING BOX LUBRICANT: TYPES 365 GT 2+2 and 365 GTC/4
   Shell Donax T6 or Veedol ATF Special 3433

STEERING BOX LUBRICANT: TYPE DINO 246 GT
   Shell Spirax EP 90

BRAKE SYSTEM: TYPES 250 GTE 2+2, 275 GTS/GTB, 330 GT 2+2, 330 GTC and 365 GT 2+2
   Shell Donax B-SAE 70 R3 or Dunlop Racing Brake Fluid

BRAKE SYSTEM: TYPES 365 GTB/4 and 365 GTC/4
   ATE Type S

BRAKE SYSTEM: TYPE DINO 246 GT
   ATE Type H

SHOCK ABSORBERS: ALL TYPES
   Shell Donax A1

SUSPENSION JOINTS: TYPES 250 GTE 2+2, 275 GTS/GTB, 330 GT 2+2, 330 GTC, 365 GT 2+2 and 365 GTB/4
   Shell Retinax A

SUSPENSION JOINTS: TYPE DINO 246 GT
   Shell Alvania EP 2

FRONT WHEEL BEARINGS: TYPES 250 GTE 2+2 AND 330 GT 2+2
   Shell Alvania 3 or Shell Retinax DX

FRONT WHEEL BEARINGS: TYPES 275 GTS/GTB, 330 GTC and 365 GT 2+2
   Shell Retinax AX

FRONT WHEEL BEARINGS: TYPES 365 GTB/4, 365 GTC/4 and DINO 246 GT
   Shell Alvania EP2

HALFSHAFT JOINTS: TYPES 275 GTS/GTB, 330 GT 2+2 and 330 GTC
    Shell Retinax A

HALFSHAFT JOINTS: TYPES 365 GT 2+2, 365 GTB/4, 365 GTC/4 and DINO 246 GT
    Molicote BR 2

Source:
<u>Operating Maintenance and Service Handbook</u> for relevant type.
<u>Ferrari Circolare Tecnica No. 162/3</u>.

One litre =	approximately 0.264 US gallon	0.220 Imperial gallon
	1.057 US quart, liquid	0.880 Imperial quart
	2.113 US pint, liquid	1.760 Imperial pint

SECTION II - ENGINE PART A - BASIC ENGINE

"A Ferrari is, above all, an engine. Without its superbly responsive, seemingly limitless-revving powerplant, a Ferrari would be just another of a number of beautiful, well-built, good handling European sports or Gran Turismo vehicles." This quote, from Warren W. Fitzgerald and Richard F. Merritt's <u>Ferrari: The Sports and Gran Turismo Cars</u> explains why, when compiling this edition of <u>Tuning Tips and Maintenance Techniques</u>, we found we had more material for the engine section than almost all the other sections combined. As a result, we have divided this section into several parts:

      A.   Basic Engine
      B.   Engine Fuel and Carburetion System
      C.   Engine Ignition System
      D.   Engine Cooling System
      E.   Engine Lubrication System
      F.   Engine Exhaust System

This first part deals with the basic engine. The principal topics are the valve system, cylinder heads and crankshafts, with miscellaneous tips on other parts of the basic engine.

VALVE TIMING SPECIFICATIONS

	INTAKE		EXHAUST	
	OPENS BEFORE TDC	CLOSES AFTER BDC	OPENS BEFORE BDC	CLOSES AFTER TDC
250 GT	22°	66°	67°	17°
250 GTE 2+2	27°	65°	74°	16°
275/2 Cam	34°	72°	66°	28°
275/4 Cam	45°	65°	60°	41°
330 GT 2+2	27°	65°	74°	16°
330 GTC	27°	65°	74°	16°
365 GT 2+2	13°15'	59°	59°	13°15'
365 GTB/4	45°	46°	46°	38°
365 GT4/BB	40°	48°	54°	26°
DINO 246	40°	52°	53°	31°
DINO 308	34°	46°	36°	38°

On two-cam engines, the two cylinder heads are in a 60° V arrangement and the valves are at an angle of 54°. They are operated by a single camshaft for each cylinder bank, by means of roller rockers with clearance setting screws.

On the 275 GT/4 Cam and 365 GT/4 Cam, the two cylinder heads are in a 60° V arrangement and the valves are at an angle of 60°. They are operated by two camshafts for each cylinder bank, one camshaft directly actuating the intake valves, the other the exhaust valves, by an inverted thimble into which fits a specially hardened spacer. Adjustment is accomplished by selecting the appropriate spacer.

On the 365 GT4/BB, the two cylinder heads are in a 180° opposed arrangement and the valves are at an angle of 46°. Actuation and adjustment is similar to that for the 365 GT/4 Cam.

On the Dino 246 and 308, the two cylinder heads are in a 65° V arrangement and the valves are at an angle of 46°. Actuation and adjustment is similar to that for the 365 GT/4 Cam.

VALVE ADJUSTMENT – TWO CAM ENGINES

It is recommended that the valve lash clearances be checked every 6,000 miles and adjusted, if necessary, to the recommended clearances.

REQUIRED MATERIALS:

    10 mm wrench or socket
    11 mm box wrench
    Torque wrench
    Small adjustable wrench
    Small piece of thin sheet metal
    Cam cover gaskets

    For 250 and 330 engines:
    .006 in (.15 mm) feeler gauge
    .008 in (.20 mm) feeler gauge

    For 275 and 365 engines:
    .008 in (.20 mm) feeler gauge
    .010 in (.25 mm) feeler gauge

CAM COVER REMOVAL:

1. Remove all acorn nuts from the cam covers.
2. Remove all flat washers from the studs.
3. Loosen, at least half way, all nuts on the chain covers.
4. Remove the bolts that secure the distributors to the cam covers.
5. Lift the ignition wire looms away from the cam covers.
6. Tap the chain covers to be sure they are loose.
7. Remove all carburetor linkages by snapping the clip from the ball joint on the rod.
8. Remove the throttle cable connection at the cam cover.
9. Remove the air cleaners if they will interfere with the removal of the cam covers (as on 330 GT 2+2s)
10. Carefully lift the cam cover off of the cylinder head. Lift upward by the black knobs on the cover. DO NOT FORCE.
11. If the cam cover hesitates, tap it with a rubber mallet to loosen.

ADJUSTMENT:

NOTE: The engine must be cold when adjusting valve clearances.

1. Crank the engine over until PM1/6 is indicated at the flywheel timing mark.
2. Intake and exhaust valves on cylinders 1 and 6 are now closed and can be checked and adjusted at this point.
3. Check the clearances between the rocker arms and the valve stems. The relevant specifi cati ons are:

For 250 and 330 engines:
.006 in (.15 mm) on intake valves .008 in (.20 mm) on exhaust valves

For 275 and 365 engines:
.008 in (.20 mm) on intake valves .010 in (.25 mm) on exhaust valves

4. The intake valves are those closest to the carburetors; the exhaust valves are those just above the exhaust pipes.

5. To adjust the clearances, loosen the 11 mm jam nut on the top of the rocker arm, insert the correct feeler gauge between the valve stem and the adjuster screw, and turn the adjuster screw with a small adjustable wrench until the feeler gauge can be removed with a slight pull – a small amount of pressure on the feeler gauge is o.k.

6. Securely tighten the jam nut, being careful not to disturb the setting of the adjuster screw. Holding the adjuster screw while lightening the jam nut should prevent this problem. Check the clearance again to determine whether or not the adjuster screw was moved. Repeat step five if the clearance is not correct.

7. Adjust one valve at a time, but adjust both the intake and exhaust valve for each cylinder before turning the engine over to adjust the next cylinder. Remember that intake and exhaust valves have different clearances – do not mix them up.

8. With a flashlight, observe the position of the cam lobe on the next cylinder to be checked. Rotate the engine until the lobe is pointing away from the rocker arm – the valve is fully closed in this position, and can be checked and adjusted.

8a. Another method of determining if the valves are closed is to turn the engine through the normal firing order and adjust each valve lifter when the piston is at TDC. Starting with cylinder 1 with PM1/6 on the flywheel mark, turn the engine slightly to the next cylinder in the firing order. The firing order on these engines is 1-7-5-11-3-9-6-12-2-8-4-10. When a piston is at TDC, both valves of that cylinder are fully closed.

9. There are two simple methods that you can use to turn the engine over between each cylinder's adjustment:
A. Connect a push-button switch from the starter fuse box to the battery. Then you can "bump" the starter and turn the engine over from under the good, while you observe the engine.
B. Jack up the rear of the car, put the gearbox in 4th (or 5th) gear, and have a helper rotate the real wheel forward while you observe the engine.

10. With either method 8 or 9, recheck each valve again to be sure you have the clearances correct. Also, double check the tightness of the jam nuts.

11. The engine can be run without reinstalling the cam covers in order to check for any noisy or sloppy adjustments. Do not run the engine at high RPM with the cam covers off or you may find oil being splashed about your engine compartment.

12. If readjustment of a particular valve clearance is indicated, be sure you wait until the engine is cold again before resetting.

REASSEMBLY

1. If the cam cover gasket appears dry, cracked, decomposed, or broken in any way, replace it with a new one. Remove the chain covers and lift the old gasket off. Avoid damaging the front circular seal and be careful not to drop any pieces of gasket into the engine. Clean the area under the gasket and remove all adhesives. Install the new gasket, carefully cutting off the small section of gasket over the distributor drive. The circular seal between the cylinder head and the chain cover should be carefully inserted through the small punched squares in the gasket. Push the gasket down on the cylinder head. Do not use adhesives to gold the gasket.

2. Clean the gasket contact area on the cam cover and the chain cover, removing all adhesives and traces of gasket material.

3. Check the oil drain holes for blockages and clean them if necessary.

4. Install the chain cover. Place a thin piece of sheet metal against the circular seal and hold it against the chain cover.

5. Using the sheet metal piece to keep the circular seal in place, carefully slide the cam cover down on the head. Slowly and carefully remove the piece of sheet metal. Apply oil if it is difficult to remove.

6. Place the flat washers on the studs, then place the four spacers on the longer studs. Fit the ignition wire looms over the proper studs. Install the 6 mm acorn nuts on all of the studs to finger tightness. Check to be sure the cam cover is down flat on the cylinder head.

7. Torque each acorn nut down to about 6 lb. ft. Tighten nuts in order from the center to the ends, working down both sides.

8. Install the distributor securing bolts and tighten them down.

9. Install the carburetor linkages and throttle cable. Do not adjust the cable taut, or you may change the idle setting.

10. Install the air cleaner if it was removed.

11. Start the engine and check it carefully for oil leaks and loose cover nuts.

CAM COVER OIL LEAKS

Dow corning makes a silicon rubber adhesive sealant called Dow 732 which is excellent for sealing rain leaks, patching leather seats, and rebuilding old rubber seals. This material is available in black, among other colors, and is highly recommended over the other brands of sealant of this type. Clean the surface to be patched with lacquer thinner before applying.

This material can also be used to prevent oil leaks around the cam covers of the engine. To apply to the engine, again clean well with lacquer thinner, then wipe the Dow 732 over the suspected leak with your finger. Allow to dry for at least three hours before starting the engine.

SEALER FOR LAMPREDI SERIES ENGINES

John Crane Plastic Lead Sealer is a high-quality pipe joint compound that can be used to seal and protect the threads and combustion sealing surfaces of Lampredi series engine cylinder barrels. Check your local plumbing supply house. Because this stuff contains lead, the Feds are forcing it to be removed from the market, so if you think you are going to need some in the future, stock up now.

CRANKSHAFT PULLEY NUT SOCKET FOR 330 SERIES ENGINES

In order to remove or tighten the 37 mm nut that fastens the pulley to the crankshaft on most 330 engines, a special socket is required. A good thinwall socket is available from Sears at a much lower cost than a factory tool. A craftsman 1-7/16 in socket with a ¾ in drive is available for less than $4.00 and with a slight modification will work quite well. Grind or file a chamfer around the outside edge opposite the drive end to allow the socket to fit down into the tapered bottom of the pulley. About 3;/8 in tapered back from the end is adequate, thus leaving a thin edge on the socket. A ¾ in to ½ in drive adaptor is needed if you do not have one.

When replacing the pulley, be sure to replace the metal locking tab and peen the ears over on the bolt head.

VALVE GUIDES AND EXHAUST SMOKE

It is probably a well-accepted fact that some Ferraris have a tendency to smoke from the exhaust. There are various reasons for this, and some basic corrective actions that can be taken to help correct or reduce this common by generally non-harmful habit.

First, and most serious, is the possibility that your Ferrari has worn rings. The only cure for this is a major overhaul.

Second, and most probable, is the proclivity for oil to leak past the valve guides. The cure for this will be taken up shortly.

Third, your carburetors may not be correctly adjusted. A too-rich mixture will add to the "idle" smoke. Fourth, you may be using too light an oil. Be sure you are using the recommended weight, or one weight heavier. A thicker oil tends to leak past the valve guides less. Valvoline has a 20W50 grade oil which will slightly reduce smoking.

Another oil alternative that is said to reduce the oil burning smoke is the use of castor oil blended for automotive use. Castor oil has the additional advantage (?) of giving off a fragrance that seems to drive automotive purists wild. A source for this oil is:
    Francisco Labs
    3015 Glendale Boulevard
    Los Angeles, CA 90039

Fifth, while on the subject of oil, be sure you are not overfilling the oil sump.

Finally, on some Ferraris the tendency to smoke is noticed only when the car is driven hard after a period of slow driving, only to have the exhaust clear up again after a few miles. This has been traced to small pockets in the heads which fill up with oil under slow running then, under hard acceleration, empty out through the valve guides.

OLD STYLE VS NEW STYLE VALVE GUIDES

Up until about mid-1966 Ferrari used bronze valve guides in their engines. Bronze valve guides are prone to wear, enlarging the valve stem hole, and allowing oil to leak down the valve stem and into the combustion chamber. As mentioned above, this is the most common cause for the characteristic Ferrari exhaust smoke.

After about mid-1966, Ferrari began using valve guides of a more durable material, and further attempted to

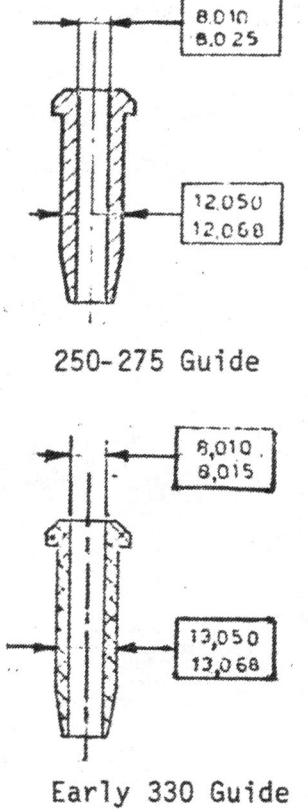

250-275 Guide

Early 330 Guide

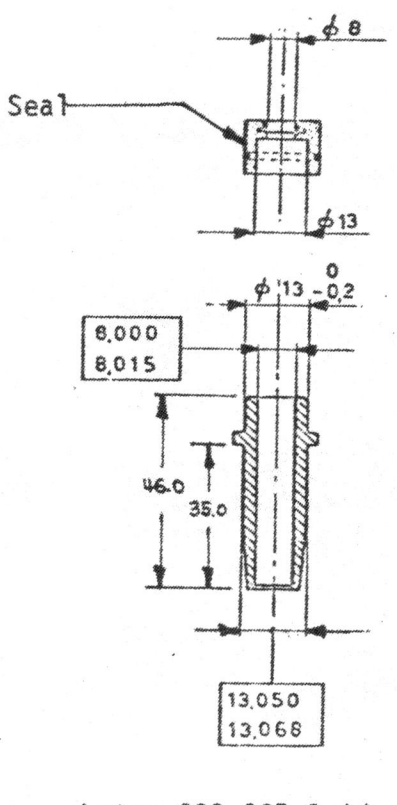

Later 330-365 Guide

stop the oil from leaking down the valve stem by installing Perfect Circle seals on the valve guides. This effectively eliminated much of the earlier problems.

So what can you do to eliminate this problem on early Ferraris?

One alternative that is especially applicable to the earlier engines is to modify the valve guides by knurling the inside diameter. This procedure is explained fully in an article by Fred Leydorf in <u>The Prancing Horse</u>, No. 36.

If you follow this procedure, be aware of the following correction:
"On page 22 of Prancing Horse No. 36, refer to figure 2. The recommendations for valve seat interference angle are interchanged. They should read:
> 1 degree for intakes with iron or steel seats
> ½ degree for exhausts and all bronze seats"

UPDATING EARLY STYLE CYLINDER HEADS

A more permanent cure is to update your old cylinder heads by replacing the worn valve guides with new style guides made of a more durable material – and preferably using the Perfect Circle rubber/Teflon seals. Such valve guides are available from several sources if you want to do-it-yourself, or any qualified shop doing Ferrari work can perform the modification for you.

FAF Motorcars, Atlanta, GA (paid advt.) is one source for such replacement guides. Their guides are specially manufactured from a very durable Aluminum-Silicon-Bronze alloy, carefully machined to very close tolerances. Since these are the replacement valve guides with which we are most familiar, what follows is based on our knowledge of these particular guides.

Installation of replacement valve guides requires modifying your existing cylinder head by machining off the post in the head.

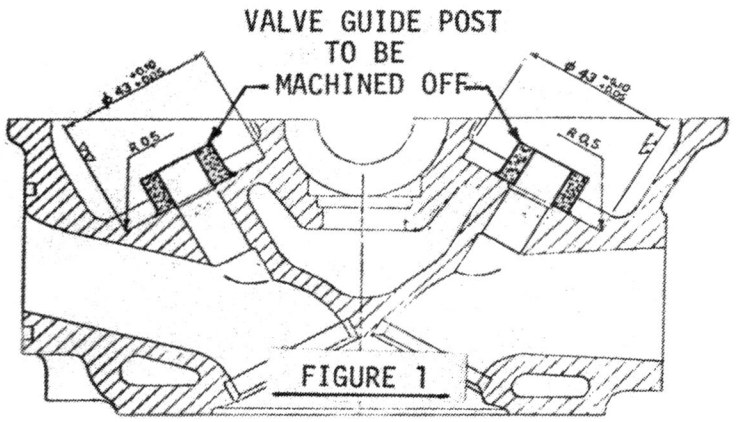

FIGURE 1

The replacement valve guides are fitted to the modified cylinder head by using a steel shim. On the later series Colombo engines – 250 outside plug, 275, and early 330 – the replacement valve guides are designed to use the Perfect Circle seals. The earlier 250 Colombo series engines' replacement valve guides do not accept the seals.

Valve guides must always be pressed in and out of the cylinder heads, never hammered. If the guide does not want to go in, a drill press and some #400 emery cloth can be used to take some excess metal off, but be careful not to take off too much.

If the bores in your cylinder head are oversize – making the valve guides fit too loosely – obtain replacement valve guides with oversize outside diameters.

After pressing the valve guides into the cylinder head, check to make sure that the inside diameter is not compressed too much. Use a .3150 in (8.000 mm) reamer to check the inside diameter. Evenly with a fairly heavy press fit, the inside diameter will rarely be reduced by more than .0002 in to .0004 in, and the reamer will act more like a plug gauge than a metal removing tool.

Finally, replacing the valve guides will not completely solve your problem if your valve stems are badly worn. Even with new guides and seals, excessively worn valve stems will still allow oil to leak past the guide and into the combustion chamber. If your valve stems are worn excessively, either replace the valves or have your present valve stems hard chromed and then machined to a finished dimension.

VALVE STEM SEALS

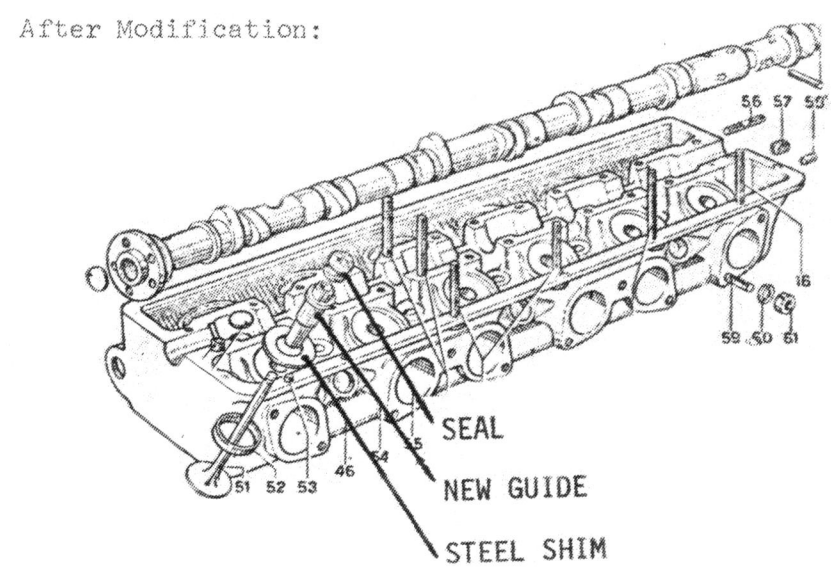

Perfect Circle seals number BAF are factory equipment on the two-cam engines, beginning with the 330 series – that were fitted with the new style valve guides. The symbol J on the seal indicates the correct 8 mm stem diameter. The other number of the seal – often BAF – is just a mold cavity number. Ignore it. See your local auto parts dealer.

These seals, when sold in an eight-cylinder engine set, are numbered 1610. There may be a six-cylinder set, which would simplify matters as then two sets would be just right for a Vee-twelve.

An inexpensive Perfect Circle tool is used for seal installation. K-D tool number 2078, slightly modified to fit the Ferrari retainer diameter, compresses the valve spring when air pressure is used in the cylinder to hold the valve shut.

VALVE GUIDE TO CYLINDER HEAD TOLERANCES

	Cylinder Head Guide Hole Diameter		Valve Guide Outside Diameter		Interference Between Mating Parts	
	mm	in	mm	in	mm	in
250-275 Bronze Guides	12.018 12.000	.4731 .4724	12.050 12.068	.4744 .4751	0.032 0.068	.0013 .0027
330 Bronze and Cast Iron Guides	13.018 13.000	.5125 .5118	13.050 13.068	.5138 .5145	Same As Above	
365 GTB/4	Same As Above		Same As Above		Same As Above	
365 GT4/BB	Same As Above		Same As Above		Same As Above	
Dino 246 GT	Same As Above		Same As Above		Same As Above	

INTAKE VALVE TO VALVE GUIDE TOLERANCES

	Valve Guide Inside Diameter		Valve Stem Diameter		Mounting Clearance		Wear Limit	
	mm	in	mm	in	mm	in	mm	in
250-275 Bronze Guides	8.010 8.025	.3154 .3160	7.995 7.980	.3148 .3142	0.015 0.045	.0006 .0018	0.08	.0032
330 Bronze Guides	8.010 8.015	.3154 .3156	Same As Above		0.015 0.035	.0006 .0014	Same As Above	
330 Cast Iron Guides w/Seals	8.000 8.015	.3150 .3156	7.990 7.980	.3146 .3142	0.010 0.035	.0004 .0014	0.10	.0040
365 GTB/4	Same As Above		7.975 7.960	.3140 .3134	0.025 0.055	.0010 .0022	Same As Above	
365 GT4/BB	Same As Above		7.975 7.940	.3140 .3126	0.025 0.075	.0010 .0030	Same As Above	
Dino 246 GT	Same As Above		Same As Above		Same As Above		Same As Above	

EXHAUST VALVE TO VALVE GUIDE TOLERANCES

	Valve Guide Inside Diameter		Valve Stem Diameter		Mounting Clearance		Wear Limit	
	mm	in	mm	in	mm	in	mm	in
250-275 Bronze Guides	8.010 8.025	.3154 .3160	7.987 7.972	.3145 .3139	0.023 0.053	.0009 .0021	0.10	.0040
330 Bronze Guides	8.010 8.015	.3154 .3156	Same As Above		0.023 0.043	.0009 .0017	Same As Above	
330 Cast Iron Guides w/Seals	8.000 8.015	.3150 .3156	Same As Above		0.013 0.043	.0005 .0017	0.12	.0050
365 GTB/4	Same As Above		7.975 7.960	.3140 .3134	0.025 0.055	.0010 .0022	Same As Above	
365 GT4/BB	Same As Above		Same As Above		Same As Above		Same As Above	
Dino 246 GT	Same As Above		7.975 7.940	.3140 .3126	0.025 0.075	.0010 .0030	Same As Above	

CYLINDER HEAD REMOVAL
WHY SHOULD YOU TAKE THE CYLINDER HEADS OFF YOUR FERRARI?

1. Because you let the car overheat, warped a cylinder head, and blew a head gasket. This happens all too frequently.

IF YOUR FERRARI IS OVERHEATING, STOP AND CORRECT THE PROBLEM.

2. Because you want to install new valve guides and seals to stop your Ferrari from smoking – see the instructions for this procedure later in the chapter.

3. Because you forgot to retorque the cylinder heads at 300 miles after taking them off for one of the above reasons, and blew another head gasket.

HOW DO YOU TAKE THE CYLINDER HEADS OFF YOUR FERRARI?

This tip comes from Dave Berg of Baltimore, MD:

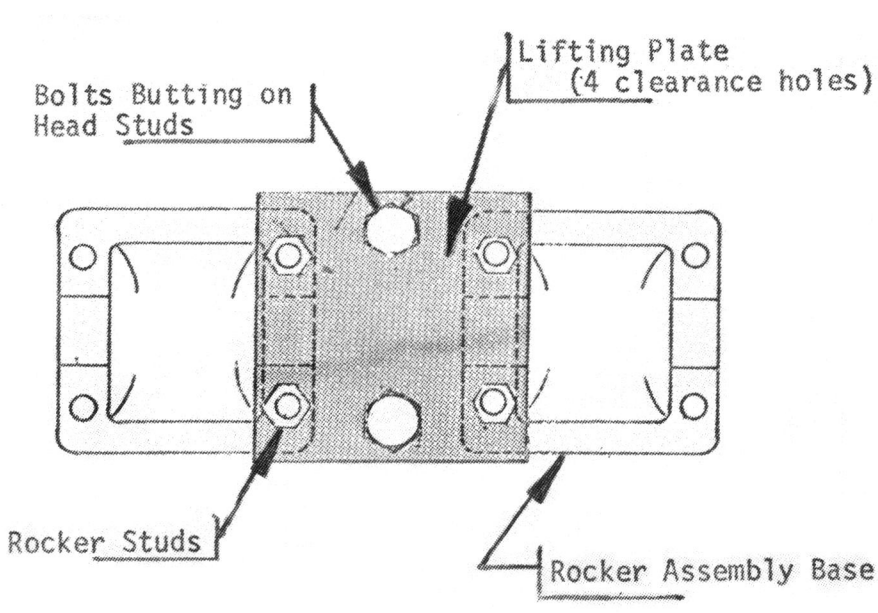

If a plate is made with four clearance holes to go over the studs which old the rocker assemblies, and with two tapped holes over the tops of the studs, then this plate can be held to the head by the rocker nuts, and with the two bolts butting against the top of the head studs, the cylinder head can be lifted off with a minimum of effort and no risk of damage from prying or hammering. Two plates will make the job easier. The bolts butting on the top of the head studs should be at least 3/8" diameter to prevent buckling.

Once this procedure is figured out, the cylinder head takes about ten minutes to remove after the nuts are all off with no damage whatsoever. Do not screw the bolts down which butt on the head studs, but use the nuts which would normally hold the rocker assemblies as this will minimize the possibility of the bolts slipping off the top of the studs and burring the threads on the studs.

CYLINDER HEAD INSTALLATION

A lengthy treatise on cylinder head installation for Colombo series engines, especially the earlier types with inboard plugs and only three studs per cylinder, can be found in <u>The Prancing Horse</u>, No. 31. This is Ferrari Club of America Technical Tip 2c-1, and was authored by Fred Laydorf. It is based on his experience with two early Colombo engines, a 1950 Type 166 and a 1954 Type 250 GT.

There are some general procedures to follow when installing cylinder heads on any Ferrari engine. First of all, whenever you install a cylinder head, always use a new replacement head gasket and <u>do not</u> apply "Permatex" or other materials to the surfaces.

The world "Alto" on the cylinder head should be installed facing upward and toward the inside of the vee – that is, toward the carburetors.

The block deck should be smooth, clean, and dry before installation.

Studs and threads should be greased or lubricated before the head is put on. Threads on the studs and nuts must be clean and fee from burrs. Washers should be flat and free from burrs – do not substitute washers and nuts other than original replacement parts.

Nuts must be brought up to the indicated torques in at least three steps, following the patterns shown on the following page. For example, if the torque specified is 60 lb. ft., on the first pass torque to 25 lb. ft., on the second pass retorque to 45 lb. ft., and then, finally, bring all nuts in their indicated sequence, up to the specified torque.

Always consult the owners manual, the workshop manual, or a <u>qualified</u> expert before attempting to torque the heads to be sure you have the correct sequence <u>and</u> torque specification.

Heads should be torqued cold.

Heads should be retorqued or checked after three hundred miles of operation.

Suggested torques are:

166, 195, 212, 225, and Early 250 GT	55 lb. ft.
250 GT Outside Plug	60/62 lb. ft.
275 GT/2 Cam	57/59 lb. ft.
275 GT/4 Cam	59/60 lb. ft.
330 FT	59/60 lb. ft.
365 GT/2 Cam	59/60 lb. ft.
365 GT/4 Cam	72 lb. ft.
Dino 246	59/60 lb. ft.

Cylinder Head Nut Torquing Sequence

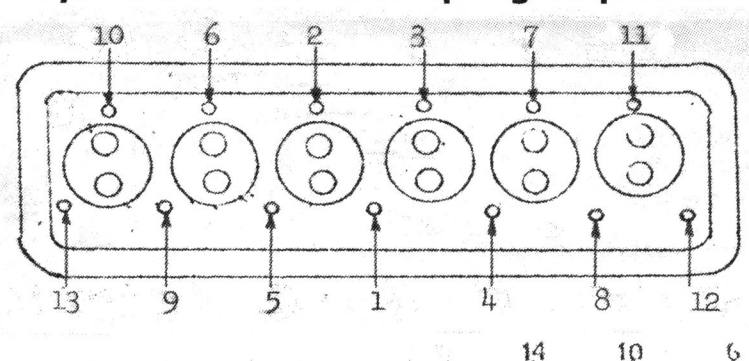

Early Colombo Series

Later Colombo Series

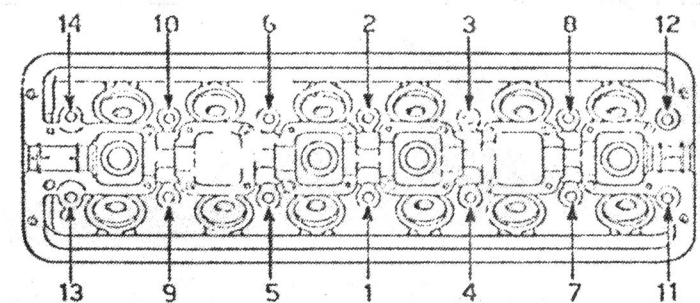

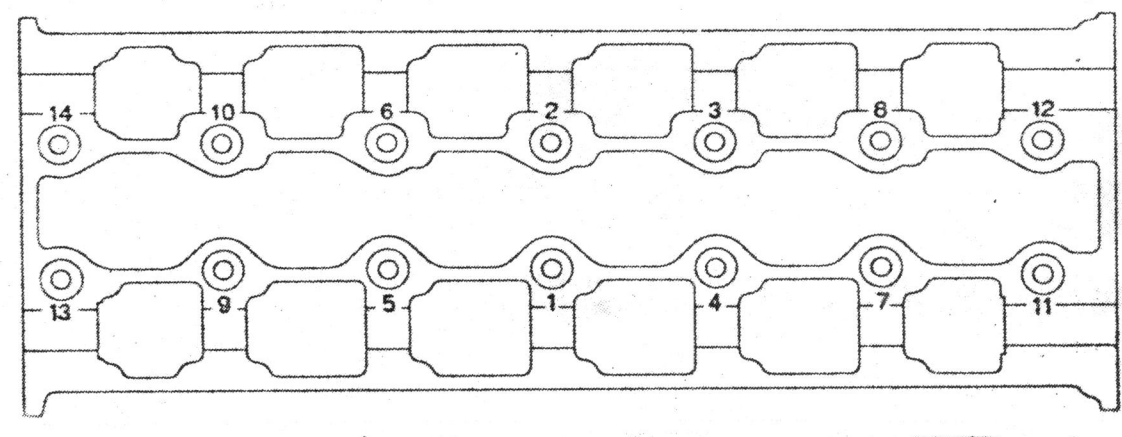

V-12 Four Cam Series

Dino V-6 Series

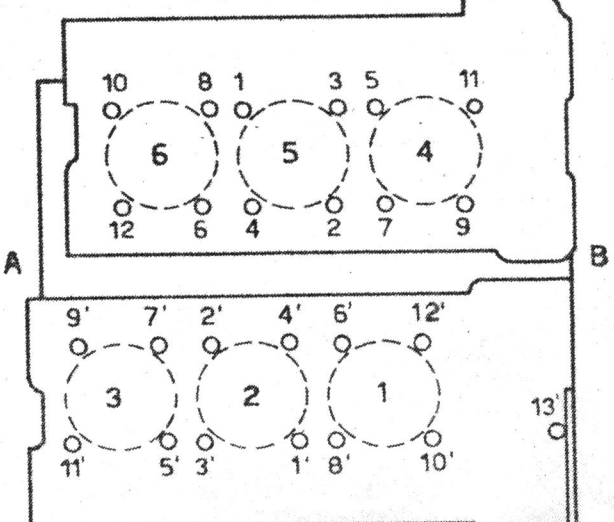

EARLY FERRARI V-12 CRANKSHAFT REGRINDING SPECIFICATIONS

TYPES 166, 195, 212, 225, and EARLY 250 GT COLOMBO SERIES (to c. 1959)

	Connecting Rod		Main	
	mm	in	mm	in
Standard	41.275	1.6249	55.000	2.1654
First regrind (.010")	41.021	1.6149	54.746	2.1554
Second regrind (.020")	40.767	1.6049	54.492	2.1454
Third regrind (.030")	40.513	1.5949	54.238	2.1354
Fourth regrind (.040")	40.259	1.5849	53.984	2.1254

TYPES 250 EU, 340, 342, 375, and 410 LAMPREDI SERIES

	Connecting Rod		Main	
	mm	in	mm	in
Standard	43.63	1.7178	59.962	2.3607
First regrind (.010")	43.37	1.7078	59.708	2.3507
Second regrind (.020")	43.12	1.6978	59.454	2.3407
Third regrind (.030")	42.87	1.6878	59.200	2.3307
Fourth regrind (.040")	42.61	1.6778	58.946	2.3207

LATER 250 GT SOLOMBO SERIES (after c. 1959)

Beginning in 1958 with the V-12 3-liter race cars (250 TR), and in 1959 with the V-12 3-liter production cars (250 GT with outside plugs), the larger Lampredi series main bearings (59.962 mm standard) were used in the Colombo series engines for additional strength. See next page.

IMPORTANT

Avoid Assumptions!! Don't take it for granted that your engine is a certain size until it is opened up and measured. Determine which undersize is needed and obtain the bearings. Install a main bearing and a rod bearing, take measurements, and regrind accordingly. This way there should be no mistakes. Exceptions to the above specifications include:

Type 166 – early models of this type had approximately 50 mm main bearings and a thick steel main bearing shell, in contrast to the later Vandervell "thin wall" inserted bearings. We have also noted at least one early Type 166 with roller bearing connecting rods.

Type 250 EU – not really an exception, but a second listing to remind you that the 250 Europa (Serial Nos. 0299 through 0351) had Lampredi series 3-liter engines and therefore have bearings of that size, in contrast to the 250 Europa GT (beginning with Serial No. 0357) which had Colombo series 3-liter engines.

There are other exceptions – but then how many of you are going to be rebuilding 375 Plus, 375 Sports, 290 MM, and early (1957) 4-cam engines?

LATER FERRARI V-12 CRANKSHAFT REGRINDING SPECIFICATIONS

	Standard	First Regrind .010"	Second Regrind .020"	Third Regrind .030"	Fourth Regrind .040"
LATER 250 GT SERIES					
Connecting Rod in.	1.6249	1.6149	1.6049	1.5949	1.5849
mm.	41.275	41.021	40.767	40.513	40.259
Main in.	2.3607	2.3507	2.3407	2.3307	2.3207
mm.	59.962	59.708	59.454	59.200	58.946
275 SERIES					
Connecting Rod in.	1.6235	1.6135	1.6035	1.5935	1.5835
	1.6241	1.6141	1.6041	1.5941	1.5841
mm.	41.238	40.984	40.730	40.476	40.222
	41.253	40.999	40.745	40.491	40.237
Main in.	2.3601	2.3501	2.3401	2.3301	2.3201
	2.3607	2.3507	2.3407	2.3307	2.3207
mm.	59.949	59.695	59.441	59.187	58.933
	59.962	59.708	59.454	59.200	58.946
330 SERIES					
Connecting Rod in.	1.7172	1.7072	1.6972	1.6872	1.6772
	1.7177	1.7077	1.6977	1.6877	1.6777
mm.	43.619	43.365	43.111	42.857	42.603
	43.632	43.378	43.124	42.870	42.616
Main in.	2.4789	2.4689	2.4589	2.4489	2.4389
	2.4794	2.4694	2.4594	2.4494	2.4394
mm.	62.966	62.712	62.461	62.204	61.950
	62.979	62.725	62.474	62.217	61.963

NOTE: When regrinding your crankshaft the original surface hardness may only be retained through the first undersize (.010"). After this it is necessary to be sure that the hardness is preserved within the specified limits (58-62 Ro). It may be necessary to nitride the crankshaft to restore the hardness. If this is done, leave the diameters oversized by .010 mm and grind them to the correct size after the nitriding process.

Once you have reached the fourth (.040") undersize on the crankshaft journals, or if your crankshaft is badly damaged, you face one of two alternatives: You can purchase a replacement crankshaft; or you can hard chrome your old crankshaft to build up the bearing surfaces, and them have them machined to size. This is only good for about .010" to .015".

250 GT TORQUE SPECIFICATIONS

Models: 250 GT and 250 GTE
Engine types: 128 and 168 – all variations (B, C, D, E, F)
Years: 1956 through 1964

RECOMMENDED TORQUES:

    Cylinder head nuts
        Inside plug engines with three nuts/cylinder   55 ft lb
        Outside plug engines with four nuts/cylinder 60/62 ft lb

    Main bearing nuts   45 ft lb

    Connecting rod nuts   35 ft lb

    Rocker assembly/cam bearing nuts   20 ft lb

    Flywheel bolts 35 ft lb

    Pressure plate bolts   30 ft lb

    Spark plugs   22 ft lb

    Bellhousing   18 ft lb

    Universal joints   18 ft lb

    Cam cover acorn nuts 5 ft lb

    8 mm engine case nuts 13/15 ft lb

    6 mm oil sump nuts   5 ft lb

NOTE: Torques indicated are for clean, lubricated threads in good condition, with air and thread temperatures between 60°F and 80°F. Flat washings must be free of all nicks and burrs to insure proper torque.

SECTION II - ENGINE PART B - ENGINE FUEL AND CARBURETION SYSTEM

The purpose of the fuel and carburetion system is to provide the engine with the combustible materials – a mixture of gasoline and air – that makes it run. One of the major problems with the carburetion system is its location. There sit the carburetors on top of the engine (at least that is where they are on most Ferraris), easily and readily accessible. In their location, they are too vulnerable to the tinkerer and uninformed do-it-yourself adjuster.

The carburetors themselves should rarely give trouble in normal operation. They have few moving parts to wear out. Their malfunctions usually occur gradually, and are most commonly caused by an accumulation of "dirt." So, when your Ferrari suddenly starts acting up with severe "carburetor" problems, It is quite often not the carburetor's fault. Before you attack the carburetors, check the ignition system, fuel delivery system, air cleaners, etc.

This part of the Engine Section deals with carburetor specifications, adjustment, and setting; tips onservicing the fuel supply system; and information on carburetor air cleaners.

CARBURETOR ADJUSTMENT

The carburetor tuning on most late model Ferraris can be accomplished without a great deal of effort even if you do not have any pervious experience with the intricacies of the carburetor di Eduardo Weber. All you need are some easy step-by-step directions, some patience, and a bit of common sense.

An interesting, informative, and also highly entertaining explanation of the necessary procedures can be found in the Ferrari Owners Club (U.S.A.) Newsletter for June 1972. This article was prepared by Herb Waxman and includes drawings explaining the finer points as well as plans for some of Herb's "special gadgets" he fabricated to make the job easier.

Another article dealing with the same subject appeared in an earlier edition of the same publication – Volume 7 No. 9 (September 1971) – this one by Ed Niles.

Finally, we come to our instructions, which were originally prepared by Jim Riff. Virtually these same instructions have appeared in the two earlier editions of this manual, and so far we have received no major complaints with them. However, be aware of the fact that these instructions were written for the 250 GT and 330 GT carburetor systems – other systems and adjustment details may differ greatly from the system described.

These instructions are for obtaining a smooth idle only and involve the adjustment of idle mixtures and throttle opening settings. High speed mixture problems or float settings are not dealt with.

PREREQUISITES:

Before attempting to adjust your carburetors, be certain that the following conditions for a smooth-running engine are present:
- Ignition timing is correct
- Spark plugs are new or in good condition
- Air cleaners are new or in clean condition
- Valve clearances are correct
- Exhaust system is free of leaks or holes
- Fuel filters are clean
- Carburetor float levels are set to specification

NOTE: On any Ferrari with disc brakes there is a vacuum line from the booster to the intake manifold. If this line develops a leak, it will affect whichever carburetor it is nearest (front or back, depending on where the vacuum line is attached to the manifold) as well as the low-speed operation of the brakes. Check this line and replace it with Gates vacuum line of the same inside diameter. You might want to go ahead and do this even if your line is not leaking since the original equipment Italian line is prone to early failure.

Before beginning the procedures to adjust your carburetors, be certain that the following conditions exist:
- Engine has just been run hard – blow out carbon, etc. Engine is warm or hot - 140°F oil temperature minimum. Weather is good – no rain or snow, no extreme temperatures.

REQUIRED MATERIALS:
  10 mm wrench
  Screwdriver with ¼ in blade
  Electronic engine tachometer
  Uni-Syn carburetor synchronizer or equivalent

PROCEDURES:

1. Close the chokes – this keeps trash and/or small bits and pieces out of the engine while you…

2. Remove the air cleaner assembly and air filters.

3. The carburetors are numbered
    No. 1 – closest to radiator (front)
    No. 2 – center
    No. 3 – closest to firewall (rear).

4. Remove the linkage clips from carburetors no. 2 and no. 3, and lift the linkage rods away from the carburetors.

5. Open the chokes, start the engine (which is still at warm operating temperature) and let it idle.

6. Increase the engine speed to approximately 1000 rpm with the throttle adjustment screw of carburetor no. 1.

7. Completely close (turn counterclockwise) the throttle adjustment screws of carburetors no. 2 and no. 3.

8. Adjust the engine speed to approximately 800 rpm with the throttle adjustment screw of carburetor no. 1.

9. Connect an electronic tachometer to one of the distributors.

    NOTE: The rpm readings on this tachometer need not be correct. You are only interested in relative readings, not accurate readings.

10. Adjust both the idle mixture screws of carburetor no. 1 until a maximum rpm indication is obtained on the electronic tachometer. Don't worry about the fact that the engine is running rough at this stage. It should be, since only one carburetor is in operation.

11. Increase the engine speed to about 3000 to 4000 rpm by "blipping" or pressing the carburetor linkage of carburetor no. 1 with your hand, then releasing the linkage, allowing the engine to return to idle. There should be no spitting or backfiring through the carburetor or crackling at the exhaust when the linkage is released. If these symptoms are present, repeat step ten with greater accuracy.

NOTE: Exhaust leaks will cause crackling at the exhaust as though the mixture were too lean.

12. Increase the engine speed to approximately 1000 rpm with the throttle adjustment screw of carburetor no. 2.

13. Completely close (turn counterclockwise) the throttle adjustment screw of carburetor no. 1. The throttle adjustment screws of carburetors no. 1 and no. 3 are now closed.

14. Adjust the engine speed to approximately 800 rpm with the throttle adjustment screw of carburetor no. 2.

15. Adjust both the idle mixture screws of carburetor no. 2 and a maximum rpm indication is obtained on the electronic tachometer. The engine will still be running rough as there is still only one carburetor in operation.

16. Increase the engine speed to about 3000 to 4000 rpm by "blipping" or pressing the carburetor linkage of carburetor no. 2 with your hand, then releasing the linkage, allowing the engine to return to idle. There should be no spitting or backfiring through the carburetor or crackling at the exhaust when the linkage is released. If these symptoms are present, repeat step fifteen with greater accuracy.

17. Increase the engine speed to approximately 1000 rpm with the throttle adjustment screw of carburetor no. 3.

18. Completely close (turn counterclockwise) the throttle adjustment screw of carburetor no. 1. The throttle adjustment screws of carburetors no. 1 and no. 2 are now closed.

19. Adjust the engine speed to approximately 800 rpm with the throttle adjustment screw of carburetor no. 2.

20. Adjust both the idle mixture screws of carburetor no. 3 and a maximum rpm indication is obtained on the electronic tachometer. The engine will still be running rough as there is still only one carburetor in operation.

21. Increase the engine speed to about 3000 to 4000 rpm by "blipping" or pressing the carburetor linkage of carburetor no. 3 with your hand, then releasing the linkage, allowing the engine to return to idle. There should be no spitting or backfiring through the carburetor or crackling at the exhaust when the linkage is released. If these symptoms are present, repeat step fifteen with greater accuracy.

22. With the engine still idling, linkages still disconnected, and the engine thoroughly warmed up, open each of the throttle adjustment screws (turn clockwise) until each carburetor contributes to an increase in engine speed.

23. Place the Uni-Syn instrument on top of carburetor no. 3. Adjust the Uni-Syn until the cork is at a readable line.

NOTE: It may be difficult to place the Uni-Syn instrument flush on the venturi due to studs, choke butterflies, etc. Either fabricate a small plastic or sheetmetal adaptor, or use a short length of 1-1/2 in. inside diameter rubber radiator hose. Be sure to push it down hard to seal any air leaks.

24. Place the Uni-Syn instrument on top of carburetor no. 1. Adjust the throttle adjustment screw until the same reading (cork level) is indicated on the Uni-Syn for carburetor no. 1 as was obtained for carburetor no. 3.

25. Place the Uni-Syn instrument on top of carburetor no. 2. Adjust the throttle adjustment screw until the same reading (cork level) is indicated on the Uni-Syn for carburetor no. 3 as was obtained for carburetors no. 1 and no. 3.

26. The engine should idle smooth at about 800 rpm. To properly adjust for this engine speed, adjust the throttle adjustment screws on all the carburetors until this rpm is indicated AND the cork levels in the Uni-Syn are the same on all carburetor venturi.

27. Stop the engine. Loosen all of the adjustments of the throttle linkage rods of carburetors no. 2 and no. 3 so that they are free to be lengthened or shortened. Loosen the actuating level arms that operate carburetors no. 2 and no. 3 so that they are free to move – these are located on the main linkage bar.

28. Place the lever arms that actuate the linkage rods so that they are in line with the lever arm of carburetor no. 1. Tighten the bolts that secure these arms.

29. Adjust the lengths of the carburetor linkage rods until they slip loosely over the ball on the lever arm. Secure the jam nuts, and replace the spring clips.

30. Start the engine. Recheck the idle – it should steady at about 800 rpm on the car's tachometer. If it does not, repeat steps twenty-two through twenty-nine.

31. Drive the vehicle in second gear at about 3000 rpm. Release the accelerator pedal and allow the engine to slow down, in gear, to 1000 rpm. There should be no crackling heard at the exhaust as the engine slows down. If crackling is heard (assuming that there are no leaks in the exhaust system), the carburetors are not correctly adjusted. Go back to the beginning and start over!!

32. If the carburetors are correctly adjusted, stop the engine, close the chokes – again to keep loose hardware out of the engine – and replace the air cleaner assembly and air filters. Finally, open the chokes.

CARBURETOR REBUILDING

The usual advice given the average Ferrari owner on the subject of rebuilding the Weber Carburetors on his Ferrari is quite simple:

"DON'T DO IT."

It is not a job for amateurs – leave it for the experts.

Now that you have been warned, if you still feel like tackling the job, a complete treatment of the subject can be found in The Prancing Horse, No. 29. This technical tip was authored by Fred Leydorf, who should know of what he speaks. Good luck.

For added clarity, be sure you also see the corrections to the above article which were published in The Prancing Horse, No. 31.

WEBER 40-DCN and 40-DFI CARBURETORS' ACCELERATOR PUMP DIAPHRAGMS
Weber 40 DCN and 40 DFI carburetors (which have been used on many popular Ferrari types since 1965) have diaphragm-type accelerator pumps. The diaphragms are Weber part no. 47407.014. They are available through Fiat dealers under Fiat part no. 9914511. This same part is used on the carburetor for a Fiat 850.

ADDITIONAL INFORMATION
If you want to learn a lot more about your Webers, we recommend two books: Weber Carburetors: Theory and Weber Carburetors: Tuning and Maintenance. Both are by John Passini. You also might want to take a look at the official Weber book, Weber Carburetors; A Technical Introduction.

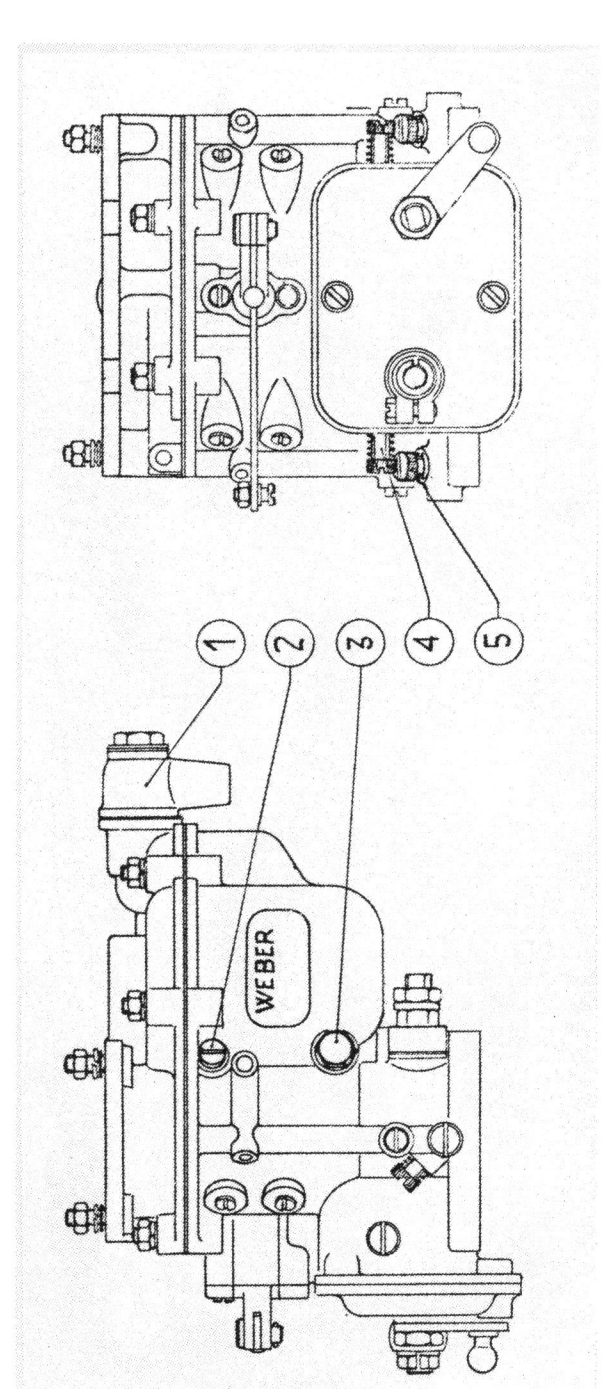

SETTING DETAILS (in mm)

	250 GTE 40DCL/6	275 GTS/GTB 40DCZ/6 40DFI/1		330 GT 40DCZ/6	330 GTC 40DCZ/6 40DFI/2		365 GT 40DFI/5	365 GTB/4 40DCN20 40DCN21		Dino 246 40DCNF/7
Choke	27.00	28.00	28.00	27.00	27.00	28.00	32.00	32.00	32.00	32.00
Main Jet	1.50	1.35	1.45	1.30	1.30	1.45	1.95	1.35	1.35	1.25
Slow Running (Idling) Jet	0.60	0.60	0.65	0.60	0.60	0.65	0.60	0.55	0.60	0.50
Pump Jet	0.60	0.60	0.65	0.60	0.60	0.60	0.60	0.40	0.40	0.50
Pump Stroke	3.00	4.50	3.00	4/4.50	4/4.50	3.00	3.00			
Central Diffusor	2.50	3.50	4.50	3.50	3.50	4.50	4.50	4.50	4.50	4.50
Air Correction Jet	1.80	2.00	1.80	1.80	1.80	1.80	2.00	1.90	1.90	2.20
Needle Valve Seat	1.75	1.75	1.75	2.25	1.75	1.75	1.75	1.75	1.75	1.75
Float Level	3/3.25	3/3.50	6/6.50	3/3.25	3/3.50	6.50	6.50	6.00	4.00	
Idle Air Correction Jet	1.40	1.25	1.25	1.20	1.25	1.25	1.25	1.20	1.20	1.20
Pump Discharge		0.50	0.50		1.00	0.50	0.50	0.50	0.50	1.00
Sump		F8	F6	F2	F8	F6	F2	F25	F25	F24

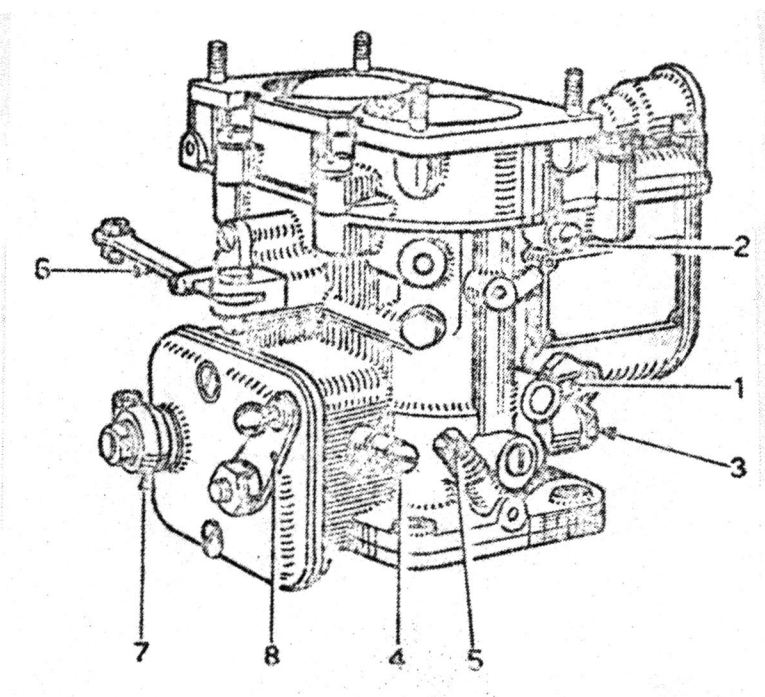

LEGEND
1. Main Jet
2. Idle Jet
3. Accelerator Pump
4. Min. Throttle Setting
5. Idle Mixture
6. Choke
7. Second Butterfly Adj.
8. Throttle linkage
9. Uni-Syn Instrument

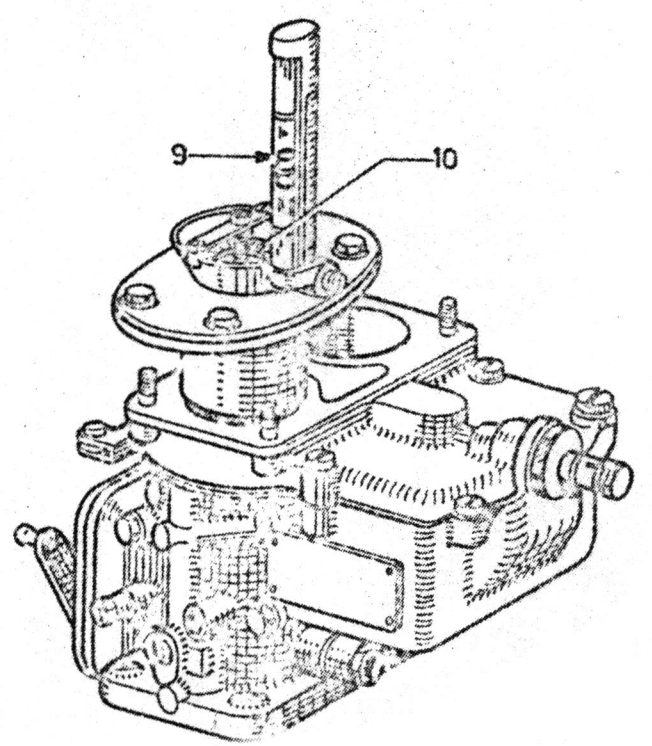

WEBER CARBURETORS
Types 36-40-42 DCF/DCL/DCZ

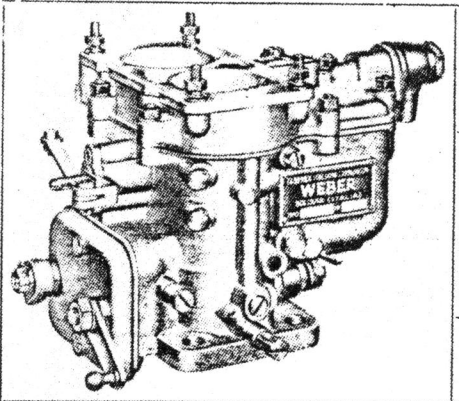

Type	twin choke downdraft
Intake pipe diameter in mm.	36 - 40 - 42
Starting device	with E.I. (E=Summer - I=Winter) control
Accelerating pump	metal piston
Extra power device	by valve
Metal	DCF: anticorodal aluminium (production ceased) / DCL: pressure cast anticorodal aluminium / DCZ: pressure cast zamac alloy

Some of the most popular installations: Alfa Romeo 1900 - Bugatti 101 - Ferrari 166/212/250/340 - Fiat 8V - Lancia Aurelia B20/B22 - Pegaso Z 102

INTRODUCTION

The double choke downdraft carburetors of the « DCF - DCL - DCZ » type are obtainable with diameters at the height of the throttle valves of 36, 40 and 42 mm. thus permitting their use over a great range of engines.

On these carburetors the device for governing the fuel mixture consists of two throttles mounted on two parallel shafts. These valves are kept in perfect relation by means of two geared segments mounted on the ends of the shafts and they open and close in counter rotation assuring a perfectly equal fuel distribution in either intake pipe.

The carburetors of the « DCF - DCL - DCZ » type are provided with an accelerating pump and starting device; moreover on request, they can be supplied with the full power device fitted. The main intake pipes of this type of carburetor work independently one from the other, since each of them constitutes a complete single choke carburetor.

DESCRIPTION

The cross section in **Figure 1**, shows how the air arrives from the top, passes through the auxiliary Venturi (2) where it mixes with the fuel coming out from the discharge tubes (3) and then, through the chokes (30) it is carried to the engine cylinders according to the opening of the throttle valves (28). From the fuel line connected with the carburetor by means of a suitable fitting, the fuel flows through the needle valve (11) into the float bowl (16) where the float (10), hinged to the pivot (13), controls the needle opening (12) and maintains the fuel level constant.

From the float bowl the fuel controlled by the calibrated main jets (22) arrives at the emulsioning tubes (4) by means of the pipes (23) from which mixed with the air arriving from the calibrated air adjusting screws (5) through the emulsioning tubes and discharge tubes (3) it reaches the carburation zone constituted by the auxiliary Venturis (2) and by the chokes (30).

The purpose of the auxiliary Venturis is to increase the vacuum around the discharge tubes (3) and to carry the emulsified fuel to the center of the chokes (30) at their narrowest diameter so as to render the mixture more homogeneous with the advantage of a better distribution to the cylinders.

For idling speed operation of the engine the fuel, by means of suitable pipes, is carried from the emulsioning tubes (4) to the calibrated idling jets (6) from which, emulsified with the air deriving from the calibrated holes (7) through the tubes (29) and the idling feeding holes (27) adjustable by means of conical screws, it arrives at the carburetor throttles chamber below the throttles where it mixes itself with the air which is sucked in by the engine vacuum through the small openings existing between the throttles chamber walls and the throttles when in idling position. From the tubes (29) the mixture arrives at the carburetor throttles chamber through the progression holes (26) situated in relation to the throttles and having the purpose of permitting smooth increase of the engine speed when starting from idle, when the throttles are opened.

The accelerating pump permits a regular increase of engine speed even when the throttles are suddenly opened.

In the carburetors of the « DCF-DCL-DCZ » type the accelerating pump is a metal piston (15) activated by the pump control shaft (8) through the lever with small roller (25) fixed to the shaft bearing the main throttles lever.

When closing the throttles, the lever (25) by means of the shaft (8) lifts up the piston (15); the fuel is then drawn from the float bowl into the pump cylinder through the intake valve (19). Opening the throttles, the shaft (8) remains free and the piston (15) is pushed towards the bottom by the spring (9); by means of the tube (17) the fuel is forced through the ball delivery valve (31) to the pump jets body (1) from which it is injected into the carburetor main intake pipes by means of suitable calibrated tubes. In order to vary the fuel quantity discharged by the accelerating pump, the carburetors of the « DCL-DCZ » type are provided with a pump exhaust screw (18); for the DCF type the exhaust is obtained by means of a suitable hole made in the pump piston (15).

In the carburetors of the « DCF-DCL-DCZ » type the ball check of the delivery valve of the accelerating pump may be substituted by a needle valve (14).

In case of special need, that is when each carburetor intake pipe feeds three cylinders or more, the carburetors of the « DCF-DCL-DCZ » type may be supplied complete with the full power device constituted by the valve (24) and calibrated jets (20). With throttles completely open the piston (15) pushed towards the bottom by the spring (9) opens the full power valve (24) allowing the fuel calibrated by the jets (20) to pass from the float bowl to the opening of the emulsioning tubes (4) through the intake valve (19) and the tubes (21) thus increasing the mixture strength drawn in by the engine through the auxiliary Venturis (2).

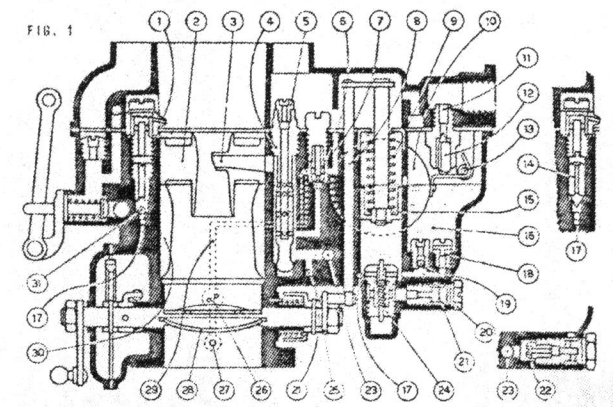

FIG. 1

DESCRIPTIVE CROSS - SECTION

1 - Pump jets body
2 - Auxiliary Venturi
3 - Discharge tube
4 - Emulsioning tube
5 - Air adjusting screw
6 - Idling Jet
7 - Idling air hole
8 - Pump control shaft
9 - Pumping prolongation spring
10 - Float
11 - Needle valve seat
12 - Needle for valve
13 - Float fulcrum pivot
14 - Needle delivery valve of pump
15 - Pump piston
16 - Float bowl
17 - Pump tube
18 - Pump exhaust screw
19 - Pump intake valve
20 - Full power jet
21 - Full power tube
22 - Main jet
23 - Jet-Emulsion tube pipe
24 - Full power valve
25 - Pump control lever
26 - Progression holes
27 - Idling hole to the intake pipe
28 - Throttle
29 - Idling mixture tube
30 - Choke
31 - Ball delivery valve

COPYRIGHT: MAY 1955 ED. WEBER

See Appendix A for enlarged text

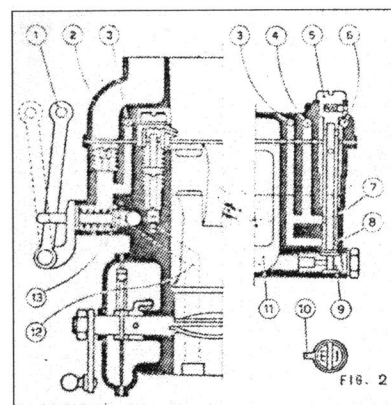

DESCRIPTIVE CROSS SECTION

1 - Starting valve control lever
2 - Starting air screw
3 - Starting mixture hole
4 - Starting air hole
5 - Starting control
6 - Air hole for starting control
7 - Hole for Summer mixture
8 - Hole for Winter mixture
9 - Starting jet
10 - Reference mark of the control on the carburetor cover
11 - Float bowl
12 - Starting mixture tube
13 - Starting valve

FIG. 2

STARTING DEVICE - Figure 2

The starting device allows a quick start when engine is cold. It is controlled from normal driving position by pulling a suitable knob on the instrument panel and should be released as soon as the engine reaches a sufficient temperature for regular running.

The fuel flowing from the constant level float bowl (11) through the calibrated jet (9) arrives at the housing tube (5) of the starting device. With the throttles in idling position the conical valve (13) is opened by the lever (1) the suction due to the engine under starter operation consists that the fuel, after a primary emulsification with the air coming through the holes (4) and (6), reaches the conical valve port (13) through the tube (3). This mixture is then further emulsified by air drawn through the calibrated screw (2) and is carried, by means of the tube (12), to the carburetor main pipes below the throttles.

For correct operation of the device it is necessary that the letter engraved upon the control (5), giving the weather conditions (E = Summer - I = Winter) should be in index with the reference finger (10) on the carburetor cover; the mixture formed by the fuel arriving from the jet (9), and the air arriving from the hole (6) is in this way fed by the calibrated hole (7) - Summer position - or by the calibrated hole (8) - Winter position - so that the device may supply the proper mixture for quick starting of the engine.

In order to allow the user to visualize the external pieces forming the carburetors of the « DCF - DCL - DCZ » type described in Figures 1 and 2, a sideview of the carburetor is shown in Figure 3 from which is seen that said pieces are easily accessible and demountable.

The carburetor being symmetrical in respect to a plane passing between the main pipes, said view denotes also the other side of the carburetor with the exception of the starting jet that, as already mentioned, is unique.

1 - Fuel filter casing
2 - Starting mixture control
3 - Idling jet
4 - Auxiliary Venturi securing screw
5 - Choke securing screw
6 - Idling mixture adjusting screw
7 - Idling speed adjusting screw
8 - Idling mixture adjusting screw
9 - Inspection screw for progression holes
10 - Main jet
11 - Full power jets
12 - Starting jet
13 - Bolt securing fuel filter casing

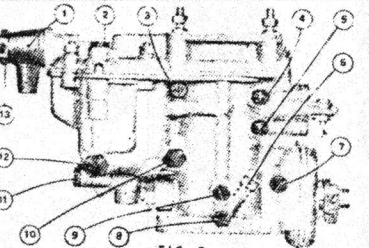

FIG. 3

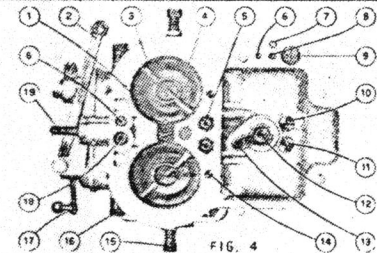

In order to indicate the position of the internal pieces of the carburetors of « DCF - DCL - DCZ » type Figure 4 shows the plan view of said carburetor without the cover.

1 - Pump jets body
2 - Starting control lever
3 - Auxiliary Venturi
4 - Chokes
5 - Emulsioning tubes complete with air adjusting screws
6 - Starting mixture tube
7 - Starting emulsion air hole
8 - Starting emulsioning tube
9 - Starting control
10 - Pump intake valve
11 - Pump exhaust screw (for DCL-DCZ only)
12 - Accelerating pump
13 - Pump control shaft
14 - Bushings for idling air
15 - Idling mixture adjusting screws
16 - Idling air adjusting screws
17 - Throttle control lever
18 - Starting emulsion air screw
19 - Starting valve

FIG. 4

TUNING FOR IDLING

In the carburetor of « DCF - DCL - DCZ » type (Figure 5) the idle adjustment device consists of the idling speed adjusting screws (1) and the mixture adjusting screws (2). The screws (1) control the amount of throttles opening synchronized by means of the geared segments; the screws (2) with the conical end maintain the proper air-fuel ratio for smooth engine operation by controlling the quantity of the mixture from the idling jets and its mixture with the air drawn in by the engine. The screws (2) can be arranged as indicated in the sketch (6) of Figure 3.

Tuning for the proper idle must be carried out with engine warmed setting first the minimum opening of the throttle valves by means of the screws (1) adjusting it to a position to prevent the engine from stalling under all conditions. Then turn the screw (2) to obtain the best mixture strength for the fastest, stable and smoothest running at that throttle valves position. Finally the throttle valves opening can then be reduced further to the most suitable idling speed.

In Figure 5 is also shown the boss (3) for the eventual connection of the automatic spark advance. For fitting on engines having said device, the carburetors of « DCF - DCL - DCZ » type can be supplied, at request, completed with said connecting piece.

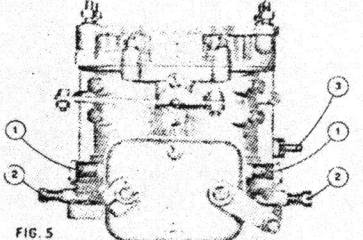

FIG. 5

OVERALL DIMENSIONS in mm.

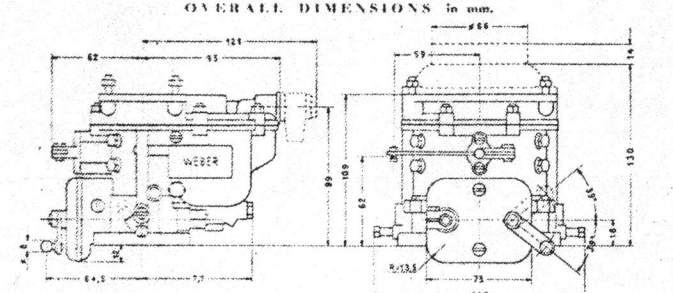

CARBURETOR FIXING FLANGES

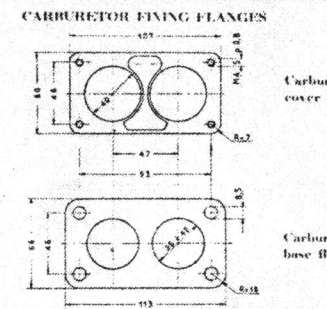

Carburetor cover flange

Carburetor base flange

Registered Office in Milan - Works: BOLOGNA, Via Timavo 33 - (ITALY)
Cable Address: WEBER - BOLOGNA - Telephone 64 573

CARBURATORI WEBER	36 DCS
CARBURATORI Tipo / CARBURETORS Type	36 DCS
Applicazione / Standard Equipment on	FERRARI 250 GT/E. 62

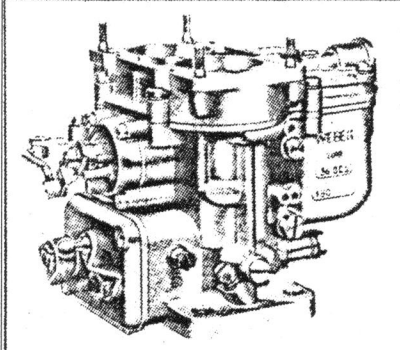

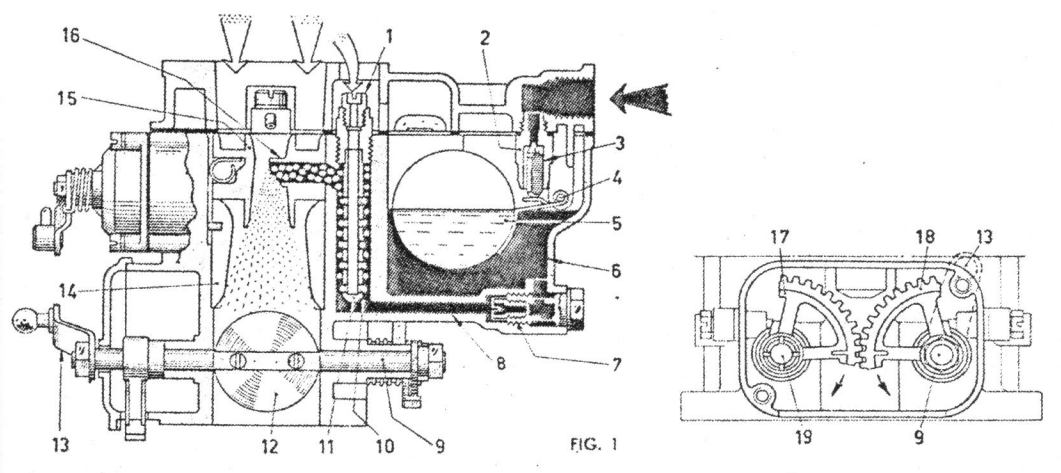

FIG. 1

MARCIA NORMALE - Fig. 1

Il carburante, attraverso la valvola a spillo (2), passa alla vaschetta (6), dove il galleggiante (5), articolato nel perno fulcro (4), regola l'apertura dello spillo (3), per mantenere costante il livello del liquido. Dalla vaschetta (6), attraverso i getti principali (7) ed i canali (8), il carburante giunge ai pozzetti (10), ove miscelato con l'aria uscente dai fori dei tubetti emulsionatori (11) e proveniente dai getti aria di freno (1), giunge attraverso i tubetti spruzzatori (16), alla zona di carburazione, costituita dai centratori (15) e dai diffusori (14).

In fig. 1 è illustrato il dispositivo per l'apertura sincronizzata delle valvole a farfalla. Agendo sulla leva (13), le farfalle (12) vengono comandate in modo sincrono mediante i settori dentati (17) e (18), fissati sugli alberini (19) e (9) e si aprono una in senso contrario all'altra, garantendo così una perfetta simmetria di alimentazione ai condotti di ammissione.

NORMAL RUNNING - Fig. 1

The fuel, through the needle valve (2) passes to the bowl (6) where the float (5), articulated in the trunnion (4), regulates the needle opening (3) in order to keep the level of the liquid constant. From the bowl (6), through the main jets (7) and ducts (8), the fuel reaches the wells (10) where, mixed with the air from the orifices of the emulsioning tubes (11) and coming from the air corrector jets (1), through the nozzles (16), it reaches the carburation area, consisting of the venturi (15) and the secondary venturi (14).

Fig. 1 shows the device for synchronized opening of the throttles. Acting on lever (13), the throttles (12) are synchronously controlled by means of toothed sectors (17) and (18) fixed to spindles (9) and (19), and open in opposite directions, so making sure of perfectly even feeding to the inlet ducts.

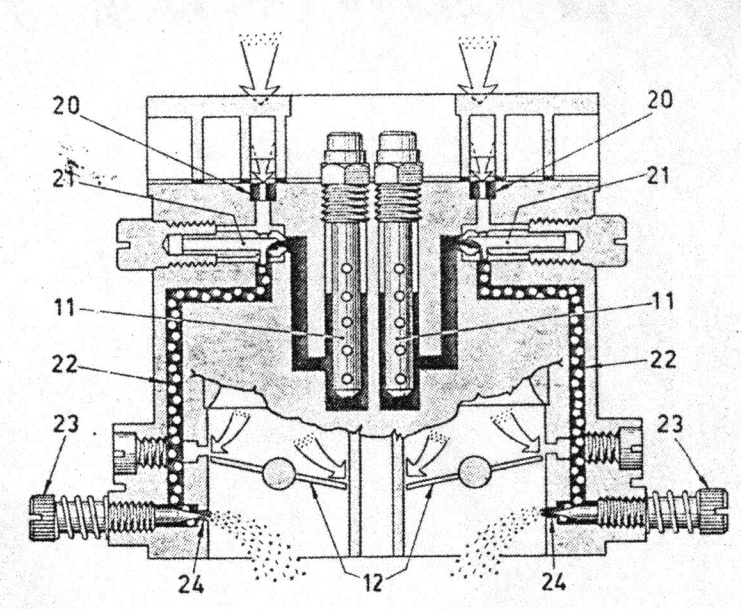

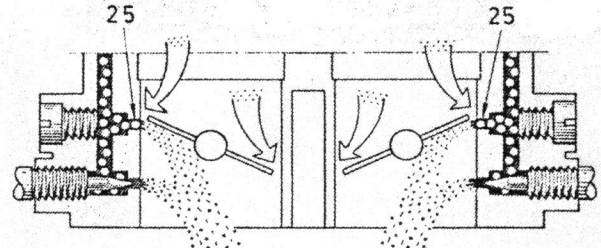

FIG. 2

MARCIA AL MINIMO E PROGRESSIONE - Fig. 2

Il carburante passa dai pozzetti, dei tubetti emulsionatori (11), ai getti del minimo (21). Emulsionato con l'aria proveniente dalle boccole calibrate (20), giunge attraverso i canali (22) ed i fori alimentazione minimo (24) registrabili mediante le viti (23) ai condotti del carburatore, a valle delle farfalle (12).

La miscela giunge ai condotti, anche dai fori di progressione (25), posti in corrispondenza delle farfalle, permettendo così un regolare aumento della velocità angolare del motore, a partire dal regime di minimo.

IDLE SPEED AND PROGRESSION - Fig. 2

From the primary emulsioning tube wells (11) the fuel passes to the idle jets (21) from which, emulsioned with the air coming from the calibrated bush (20), through ducts (22) and the idle feed orifices (24), the last being adjustable by means of screws (23), it reaches the carburetor ducts downstream of the throttles (12).

The mixture also reaches the ducts from progression holes (25) placed on a level with the throttles, so allowing a regular increase in angular speed of the engine starting from idling speed.

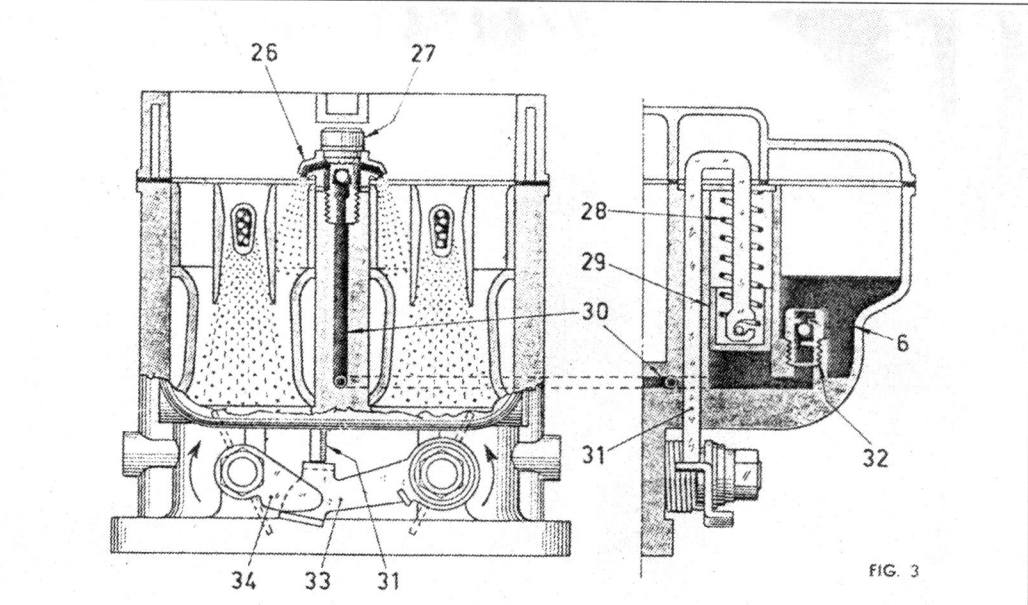

FIG. 3

FUNZIONAMENTO IN ACCELERAZIONE - Fig. 3

Chiudendo le farfalle, la leva (33), tramite l'asta (31) solleva lo stantuffo (29); il carburante viene aspirato dalla vaschetta (6) nel cilindro della pompa, attraverso la valvola di aspirazione (32).

Aprendo le farfalle, la leva (34) abbassa la leva (33), liberando l'asta (31). Lo stantuffo (29), sotto l'azione della molla (28), viene spinto verso il basso; mediante la conduttura (30) il carburante viene iniettato attraverso la valvola (27) ed i tubetti tarati del getto pompa (26) nei condotti del carburatore.

La valvola di aspirazione (32), può essere provvista di un foro laterale calibrato, che scarica in vaschetta l'eccesso di carburante.

ACCELERATION - Fig. 3

Closing the throttles, lever (33), through the rod (31), raises the plunger (29). The fuel is drawn from the bowl (6) into the cylinder of the pump through the inlet valve (32). By opening the throttles, lever (34) lowers lever (33), so freeing rod (31). The plunger (29), through the action of spring (28), is pushed downwards; along the ducts (30) the fuel is injected through valve (27) and the calibrated pipes of the jet pump (26) into the carburetor ducts.

The inlet valve (32) may be supplied with a lateral calibrated orifice which discharges any excess fuel into the well.

MISURE D'INGOMBRO in mm.	OVERALL DIMENSIONS in mm.

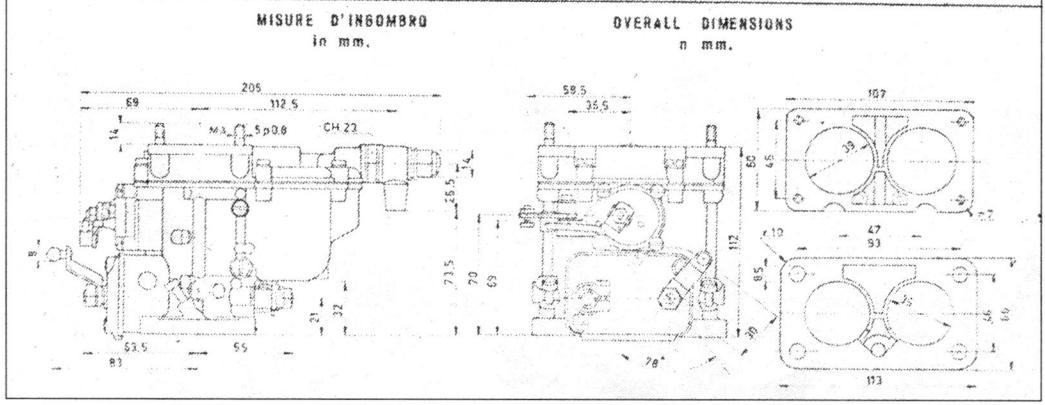

See Appendix A for enlarged text

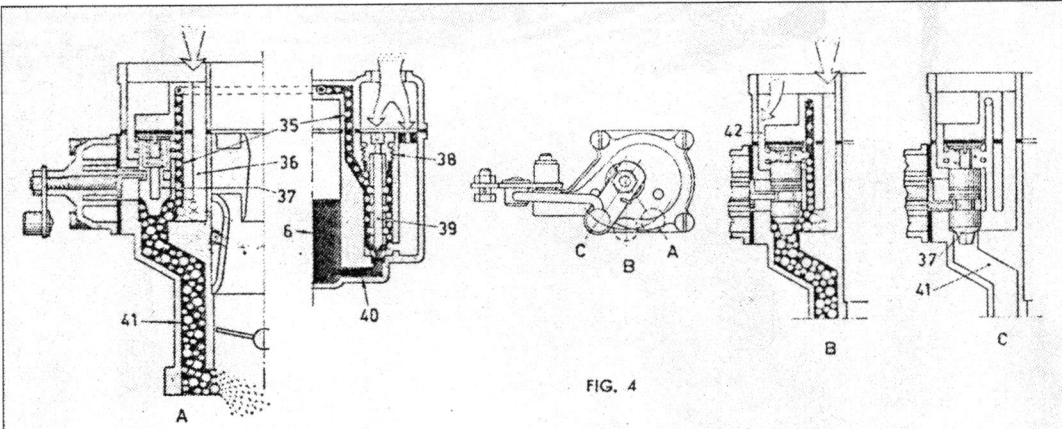

FIG. 4

DISPOSITIVO DI AVVIAMENTO Fig. 4

Il carburante, dalla vaschetta (6), passa al dispositivo di avviamento, attraverso il canale (40) ed il getto avviamento (39). Emulsionato con l'aria calibrata dal getto aria di freno (38) proveniente dalla presa d'aria del carburatore giunge al vano dello stantuffo (37), attraverso il canale (35), ove si miscela con l'aria proveniente dal canale (36). La miscela così formata, viene aspirata attraverso il canale (41), permettendo un pronto avviamento del motore. (Schema A)

Ad avviamento ottenuto, disinserire parzialmente il dispositivo di avviamento. (Schema B)

In queste condizioni, un ulteriore afflusso di aria proveniente dal canale (42), smagrisce il titolo della miscela erogata dal dispositivo di avviamento, permettendo un regolare funzionamento del motore a freddo.

Riscaldandosi però il motore, detta miscela risulta a titolo troppo ricco ed in quantità eccessiva; pertanto è necessario escludere progressivamente il dispositivo di avviamento, con l'aumentare della temperatura del motore.

Con il dispositivo di avviamento disinserito, lo stantuffo (37) chiude il canale (41), impedendo il richiamo di miscela. (Schema C)

NORME DI IMPIEGO DEL DISPOSITIVO AVVIAMENTO

Per ottenere dal dispositivo avviamento, tutti i vantaggi che esso può fornire, si riassumono le norme di impiego, che è opportuno osservare.

AVVIAMENTO DEL MOTORE

Avviamento a freddo. Inserire completamente il dispositivo di avviamento. Posizione «A». Ad avviamento ottenuto ridurre il grado d'inserzione.

Avviamento a motore semicaldo. In questo caso è sufficiente inserire parzialmente il dispositivo di avviamento. Posizione «B».

Messa in efficienza del veicolo. Durante il periodo di riscaldamento del motore, anche con veicolo in moto, disinserire progressivamente il dispositivo con manovre successive, in modo da avere sempre una erogazione di miscela supplementare strettamente necessaria per un regolare funzionamento del motore. Posizione «B».

Marcia normale del veicolo. Non appena il motore ha raggiunto una temperatura sufficiente per un regolare funzionamento, escludere il dispositivo di avviamento. Posizione «C».

STARTING DEVICE - Fig. 4

The fuel passes from the bowl (6) to the starting device through duct (40) and the starting jet (39). Emulsioned with the air coming from the carburetor air intake (calibrated by the air corrector jet (38) it reaches the plunger chamber (37), through duct (35), where it is mixed with air from duct (36); this mixture is then aspirated through duct (41), so permitting ready starting of the engine. (Diagram A).

As soon as the engine is started, partially close the starter device. Diagram B).

In these conditions a further airflow, from duct (42) leans the mixture delivered by the starter, so permitting normal working with a cold engine.

As the engine warms up, however, this mixture is too rich and in excessive supply, so the starting device must be progressively cut out as the temperature of the engine rises.

With the starting device disconnected, the plunger (37) closes duct (41) stopping the call for mixture. (Diagram C).

INSTRUCTIONS FOR USE OF STARTING DEVICE

In order to get the best results possible from the starting device, the most important instructions for use are summarised below:

ENGINE STARTING

Starting from cold - Fully insert the starting device. Position «A». On starting, reduce its degree of connection.

Starting with engine warm - Partial insertion of the starting device is all that is needed in this case. Position «B».

Putting the vehicle to work - During warming-up of the engine, even with the vehicle in motion, progressively disconnect the device with successive manipulations so as to have always a supplementary distribution of mixture, sufficient but no more than necessary for normal functioning of the engine. Position «B».

Normal running of the vehicle - As soon as the engine has reached a temperature sufficient for normal running, cut out the starting device. Position «C».

Soc. p. Az. EDOARDO WEBER - Fabbrica Italiana Carburatori
Stab. / Works: BOLOGNA - Via Timavo 33 - Telef. 41.79.95 (Italy) TELEX: 51119 WEBER BO
Ind. Telegrafico / Cable Address: WEBER - BOLOGNA

FUEL SYSTEM

WATER IN FUEL TANK AND FUEL LINES

Water can find its way into the fuel tank and fuel lines by various means – condensation, leakage in rainy weather, or, as one owner reports, through the extra-large Le Mans-type fuel filler when refueling on a rainy day. This water can cause real problems in freezing weather by getting to the gas filter, the fuel lines, the electric fuel pump, etc. and freezing. Anyone who drives his Ferrari in freezing weather should drain his gas tank and filters at least twice during the winter season. The amount of water and other unwanted material that comes out can be astounding.

A word of caution before you drain your fuel tank – be sure it is nearly empty. This means double-checking the capacity of your tank. It is not always sufficient to just rely on your fuel gauge or warning light to tell you when the tank is empty. On some cars these indicate the tank is empty when there is still a reserve fuel supply in the tank.

Before draining the gas tank, be sure you have a new gasket for the drain plug. On some Ferraris the plug in the fuel tank is the same size as the crankcase drain plug, so the gasket for one will work for the other.

UNFILTERED FUEL LINES

Fuel lines on many very early Ferraris are sometimes unfiltered. The filter is usually found in the area of the electronic booster pump line. By splicing in an AC gasoline filter (in-line type_ such as a GF61P in series with this line, additional contamination can be trapped.

LEAKING FUEL LINES

If a fuel leak develops in the flexible fuel lines that connect to the carburetors, try replacing them with standard 3/8 in inside diameter neoprene fuel line. Remove the brass banjo assemblies from the old hoses and screw them into the new neoprene hose. For added safety, add a screw-type hose clamp.
It is a good idea to regularly inspect all fuel lines as the original equipment lines tend to "dry out" and crack.

An excellent investment is a 2-3/4 lb fire extinguisher, carried in the car at all times. A leaking fuel line can cause a disastrous fire.

FUEL PUMPS

Early Ferraris (1950-1955) use pairs of diaphragm-type fuel pumps. Tips on rebuilding these pumps appeared in <u>The Prancing Horse</u>, No. 31.

Internal parts for early Fispa fuel pumps are available from Doug Heinmuller, Box 565, McDonough Road, Baltimore, MD 21208. Diaphragms for these pumps carry his part no. 29 PX and cost about $5.00 each.

AIR FILTERS

Some hints for buying new air filter elements:

If at all possible, take your old element along with you when you go to buy a new one, especially if you are trying to find a substitute filter element. This way you can compare the old with the replacement.

If you can't take the old one along, or if you are ordering by mail, measure your old element and compare the measurements with the replacement element, or mail the measurements with your order. The critical dimensions are inside diameter, outside diameter, and height on round filters, or height, length, and thickness on the flexible elongated oval type. Some Ferraris use small oval filters – you may have to buy round filters and ovalize them to fit.

Major problems are the 330, 275/2 cam and 365/2 cam engines which were fitted with a truly eclectic range of air cleaner assemblies.

Some reported acceptable substitute air filter elements include:

For the 250 GT Berlinetta Lusso and, we assume, other 250 GTs of the same era, Hastings part no. AF-24 is reputed to be an exact duplicate air filter. These low-cost American made filters are stocked by most large parts dealers.

It is also alleged that the air filter element for the Fiat 1100 will work on the Lusso.

330GT 2+2 air filter elements are supposed to be the same as those used on the Fiat 850, which would also mean that Fiat 850 air filter elements should fit some 275/2 cam and early 330 GTC and GTS engines.

Please be careful, when attempting to find substitute air filter elements, to follow the hints for buying new elements that are listed above.

Finally, Fram paper element replaceable type air filter elements, and Fispa cleanable semi-permanent type air filter elements to fit most Ferraris are available from FAF Motorcars, Atlanta, GA.

SECTION II - ENGINE PART C - ENGINE IGNITION SYSTEM

The ignition system's purpose is to provide the spark that ignites the combustible mixture provided by the carburetion system. This is more complex than it sounds, since it involves converting low voltage to high voltage and varying the timing of the spark to suit varying engine speeds.

The ignition system is one specialized component of an overall electrical system that depends on a storage battery and alternator for current. However, in this section we will deal strictly with the specialized ignition component, and take up the rest of the electrical system later.

This part of the Engine Section deals with spark plugs; distributor specifications, timing, and maintenance; and miscellaneous tips on the ignition system.

SPARK PLUGS

When choosing spark plugs for your engine, always use a plug of the recommended heat range. A plug with a too hot tip temperature can burn a hole in your piston.

When installing spark plugs, use a good high temperature grease, such as Molykote, on the threads. Do no over-tighten the plugs. The factory recommended torque specifications of 22 ft lb for the spark plugs in most V-12 engines; with the 365 GT/4 cam series they recommend 27.5 ft lb.

If you strip the threads in a spark hole, a Helicoil insert can help salvage the head. Check with your local automotive machine shop for details.

It is normal for spark plugs to increase their gap during usage. You should pull the plugs for inspection and regapping several times between changes.

Spark plugs should be replaced at 6000-mile intervals.

RECOMMENDED SPARK PLUGS

On early V-12 engines – up through the 330 GT 2+2 Mark 1 and the 275 GTS/GTB – the recommended plug was the Marchal 34 HF. The Champion equivalent of this plug was the N-3.

On later V-12 engines, the recommended plug was the Champion N-6Y. This same plug (and not the Champion N-6m as sometimes indicated) is a suitable replacement for the Champion N-3, provided a 1 mm copper washer is installed to increase the plug's clearance.

Other spark plugs that are equivalent to the Champion N-6Y are:
    AC   438 XLS or 41XLS
    Autolite   AG902
    Bosch W280T30
    KLG   FE-125P
    Marelli CW 89 LP
    NGK   B-7ES

The recommended gap setting for plugs installed in a Ferrari V-12 engine is 0.5 to 0.6 mm or 0.2 to 0.25 in.

The Dino 206 and 246 use Champion N-60Y spark plugs, with a recommended gap of 0.4 to 0.5 mm or 0.16 to 0.20 in.

The Dino 308 uses Champion N-6Y spark plugs, with a recommended gap of 0.5 to 0.6 mm or 0.20 or 0.25 in.

DISTRIBUTORS

From the later 250 GT Inside Plug Series V-12 through the 365 GTB/4 V-12, the standard equipment distributors on Ferraris have been two Marelli type S-85A or S-85AA six cylinder distributors. Some early 250 GT Inside Plug V-12s, and more recently the 365 GTC/4 V-12, were fitted with only one twelve cylinder distributor.

One important exception to this general rule is the fact that there were some 275 GTB/4s fitted with Marelli S-85E distributors. The S-85E has a fixed advance of 24°, while the S-85A has a fixed advance of 10°. There were some early examples of this engine fitted with S-85E distributors but with flywheels referenced for 10° fixed advance (AF).

IGNITION POINTS

Ignition point sets for S-85A distributors are Marelli part no. H.710071.02. Suitable substitution ignition points, other than original factory equipment, are no available – at least we don't know of any.

If you live near an ignition parts manufacturer, or have a good friend in the auto parts business, you might be able to get new tungsten tips mounted on a set of breaker points.

The recommended ignition point gap is 0.35 mm or 0.014 in.

It is advisable to replace the points on your Ferrari every 15,000 miles. If you are not the original owner of your car, and do not know how many miles your points have accumulated, you should change them as soon as possible. It is quite common for point springs to break after extended mileage.

We also recommend that you carry a spare set with you at all times. Points are quite easy to obtain and relatively inexpensive – until yours happen to break when you are on a trip.

DISTRIBUTOR ROTOR

The rotor for Marelli S-85A distributors is Marelli part no. 703880.01. The above comments concerning replacement, failure, and carrying a spare apply equally as well to the distributor rotors.

DISTRIBUTOR WIRING

The high tension wires from the distributors to the spark plugs should be periodically checked to be sure they have not become ineffective due to loose connections or having developed high resistance. Because of the smoothness of the V-12 Ferrari engine, the loss of one or two plugs is often not noticed in normal driving.

To check for faulty spark plug leads, try the Sears high voltage meter, which costs less than $13.00. This gives a true indication of high voltage output at each point of the ignition system.

It is also advisable to replace your spark plug leads every 25,000 miles or five years. This will help avoid problems of high resistance leads and will short-circuit (pun intended) wet-weather starting problems. Spark plug leads should contain stranded wire conductors with hypolon or silicon insulation. Spark plug terminals should be soldered to the wire after crimping. Use silicon rubber spark plug boots unless Rajah type terminals are used – these do not require boots.

The ignition wiring of distributors is quite easy, but do not be confused by the numbers on the distributor caps. These numbers, 1 to 6, are the firing order of the distributor, <u>not</u> the firing order of the engine. The correlation is as follows:

RIGHT BANK		LEFT BANK	
Number on Cap	Plug Number	Number on Cap	Plug Number
1	1		
		1	7
2	5		
		2	11
3	3		
		3	9
4	6		
		4	12
5	2		
		5	8
6	4		
		6	10

Complete firing order: 1-7-5-11-3-9-6-12-2-8-4-10

DISTRIBUTOR ROTOR SHAFT BEARING

Periodically check your distributor rotor shaft for free play. Remove the distributor cap and rotor. Hold the shaft between your fingers and push sideways or wiggle horizontally. If free play is noted, a worn bearing is probably the cause. To replace the bearing, remove the three screws from the bearing support and lift it out. Using a bearing puller, gently pull the exposed bearing off the shaft. Replace the bearing with a new SKF no. R8-2RSJ.

IGNITION COIL

To check the performance of your Marelli ignition coil, use an ammeter or an ohmmeter. The relevant specifications are:

Current drain through ignition coil and ballast resistor = 5A at 13V

Current drain of ignition coil only = 10A at 13V

Ballast resistor ohmmeter reading = 1.50 to 1.90 ohms

Coil primary resistance (D to +) = 1.30 to 1.60 ohms

Coil secondary resistance (D to HV) = 12,000 ohms

There should be no resistance measured between any terminal and the metal shell of the coil (all leads disconnected).

If the Marelli coil checks out as defective, a Delco ignition coil from a late-model Chevrolet six cylinder will exactly replace the original. Just mount the ballast resistor on the coil and connect it to the harness. The capacitor on the distributor will retain the same value - .18 MFD.

IGNITION CAPACITOR

Ignition point capacitors from most General Motors vehicles (but only GM vehicles) can be substituted for the Ferrari Marelli capacitor. These capacitors are all .18 MFD, which is what is required. Choose one that will mount the easiest – consider lead length, etc.

DISTRIBUTOR TIMING CHECK

To check the ignition timing on two-cam V-12 engines, follow these procedures:

1. Remove the inspection plate on top of the bellhousing.

2. Clean all markings on the flywheel with solvent.

3. Connect an electronic strobe timing light to cylinder no. 1 (on the right bank).

4. Start the engine and allow it to idle below 1000 rpm.

5. Aim the timing light into the inspection port above the flywheel. 10AF should be near the fixed pointer.

6. Increase the engine speed to 5000 rpm. 42AM should now be indicated.

7. Stop the engine and connect the timing light to cylinder no. 7 (on the left bank).

8. Start the engine and allow it to idle below 1000 rpm.

9. Aim the timing light into the inspection port above the flywheel. 10AF should be near the fixed pointer.

10. Increase the engine speed to 5000 rpm. 42AM should now be indicated.

11. If any adjustment is required, follow the distributor timing procedures below.

DISTRIBUTOR TIMING

To completely time a late model V-12 Ferrari, follow these procedures:

REQUIRED MATERIALS:

Electronic strobe timing light
14 mm wrench
.014 in (.35 mm) feeler gauge

PREREQUISITES:

Before attempting to time your Ferrari, be sure these conditions are present:
Points should be new or, if old, in good condition. File old points with an ignition point file so that a smooth parallel surface remains. Point gaps should be checked and set to the recommended .014 in.

PROCEDURES:

1. Remove the inspection plate on top of the bellhousing. NOTE: To avoid removing the cover plate on the bellhousing, substitute a clear plastic (preferably an unbreakable Lexan one) plate for the metal plate.

2. Make sure the markings on the flywheel are readable. If necessary, clean them with solvent.

RIGHT BANK:

3. Connect an electronic strobe timing light to cylinder no. 1 (on the right bank).

4. Start the engine and allow it to idle below 1000 rpm.

5. Aim the timing light into the inspection port above the flywheel. The 10AF mark which is just before the PM1/6 mark on the flywheel should be near the fixed pointer.

6. Increase the engine speed to 5000 rpm. The 42AM mark which is 42° before the PM1/6 mark on the flywheel should be near the fixed pointer.

7. If the 42AM does not line up with the pointer, loosen the 14 mm nuts holding the distributor top to the base just enough to allow the distributor top to be moved. Rotate the distributor top until the 42AM lines up with the pointer. Retighten the 14 mm nuts.

    NOTE: It is more important that the timing be correct at high speed than at idle speed. Therefore, if the 42AM lines up, and the 10AF is within 2° of lining up, that is good enough. If the discrepancy is more than this, check the advance mechanism in the distributor base and all the distributor bearings for wear.

8. Stop the engine and connect the timing light to cylinder no. 6 (on the right bank).
9. Start the engine and increase its speed to 5000 rpm. The same 42AM mark (now 360° later)

should be near the fixed pointer.

10. If the 42AM does not line up with the pointer, stop the engine and adjust the position of the second "even cylinder" set of points by loosening the two screws and sliding the set forward or backward, thereby timing the even numbered cylinders.

    NOTE: To determine which points control the even and the odd numbered cylinders, turn the engine over until the rotor points to no. 1 on the distributor cap. The set of points that are just opening are the odd numbered set (the flywheel should be just coming up to the 10AF mark also). This "odd set" is not adjusted for timing purposes, only the "even set" is moved to adjust the cylinder no. 6 firing position.

11. This completes the timing of the right cylinder bank. Be sure to check the tightness of the 14 mm distributor nuts and the point screws.

LEFT BANK:

12. Connect the timing light to cylinder no. 7 (on the left bank).

13. Start the engine and allow it to idle below 1000 rpm.

14. Aim the timing light into the inspection port above the flywheel. The 10AF mark which is just before the PM7/12 mark on the flywheel should be near the fixed pointer.

15. Increase the engine speed to 5000 rpm. The 42AM mark which is 42° before the PM7/12 mark on the flywheel should be near the fixed pointer.

16. If the 42AM does not line up with the pointer, loosen the 14 mm nuts holding the distributor top to the base just enough to allow the distributor top to be moved. Rotate the distributor top until the 42AM lines up with the pointer. Retighten the 14 mm nuts.

    NOTE: Again, it is more important that the timing be correct at high speed than at idle speed.

17. Stop the engine and connect the timing light to cylinder no. 12 (on the left bank).

18. Start the engine and increase its speed to 5000 rpm. The same 42AM mark (now 360° later) should be near the fixed pointer.

19. If the 42AM does not line up with the pointer, stop the engine and adjust the position of the second "even cylinder" set of points by loosening the two screws and sliding the set forward or backward, thereby timing the even numbered cylinders.

    NOTE: To determine which points control the even and the odd numbered cylinders, follow the directions in the note under step no. 10 above, using cylinder no. 7 rather than cylinder no. 1

20. This completes the timing of the right cylinder bank. Be sure to check the tightness of the 14 mm distributor nuts and the point screws.

21. It is always wise to repeat the distributor timing check after adjusting the timing to double check your accuracy.

At least one person, when attempting to follow the above directions, found them "somewhat confusing" – actually, he was referring to the directions which appeared in one of the earlier editions and we hope some of that confusion has been cleared up. This same Ferraristi, who does his own maintenance work on his Ferrari, proceeded to write a good set of procedures for an alternate "static" timing method. These instructions, authored by Thomas W. Herrin, Jr., can be found in The Prancing Horse, no. 37.

DISTRIBUTOR POINT SYNCHRONIZATION

This tip comes from Dudley Kuhlman of Columbus, OH:

In order to do an accurate job of point synchronization, you need to make yourself a distributor holder so you can take the distributor out of the car and have it on the bench, mounted solid so there is no rocking, but where you are still able to turn the bottom of the shaft. You will also need a degree wheel, a pointer, and a self-powered timing light.

The degree wheel can be made from one of the smaller types used for crankshafts. They are usually 6, 7 or 8 inches in diameter, and can often be bought in a good Hot Rod shop. Then have someone with a lathe cut the inside out so it just fits over the distributor with the cap off, and put in a centering pin hole so the degree wheel can't turn.

The pointer must fit well on the distributor shaft, and can be spring-over type. It should be long enough to reach out to the edge of the degree wheel. It will be more accurately read if it has a right angle end.
The timing light should be the "flashlight" type with two wires which plug into the base. McCullough dealers are one possible source for the required type of light.

The procedure is thus: Set the point gap on both sets of points (.014 in). Then put the degree wheel in place, attach the pointer, and hood one lead from the timing light to the high voltage outlet on the side of the distributor, and the other lead to the ground.

Turn the shaft until the light goes on (or off, depending upon which way you want to do it, but once you pick one, remain constant). Continue to turn the shaft, seeing if the light goes on (or off) every sixty degree. If not, some adjusting is in order.

Depending upon what kind of reading you are getting, it may be necessary to move one or both sets of points. This can be done easily enough without disturbing the original point gap setting. Once you have the new position secure, check it again with the light and degree wheel. It takes time and patience to get it right, but it is possible to come out with it set up so you have the points synchronized at 60° all the way around.

Once the distributor is set up on the bench, go back to the car, bring the 10AF mark on the flywheel for the bank you are working with into line with the fixed pointer, put the distributor back on, and with the same timing light hooked up to the high voltage lead, rotate the distributor body until the light just comes on (goes off). Secure the nuts holding the body and you should be "On Time". Repeat for the other distributor.

Finally, check the timing with the engine running.

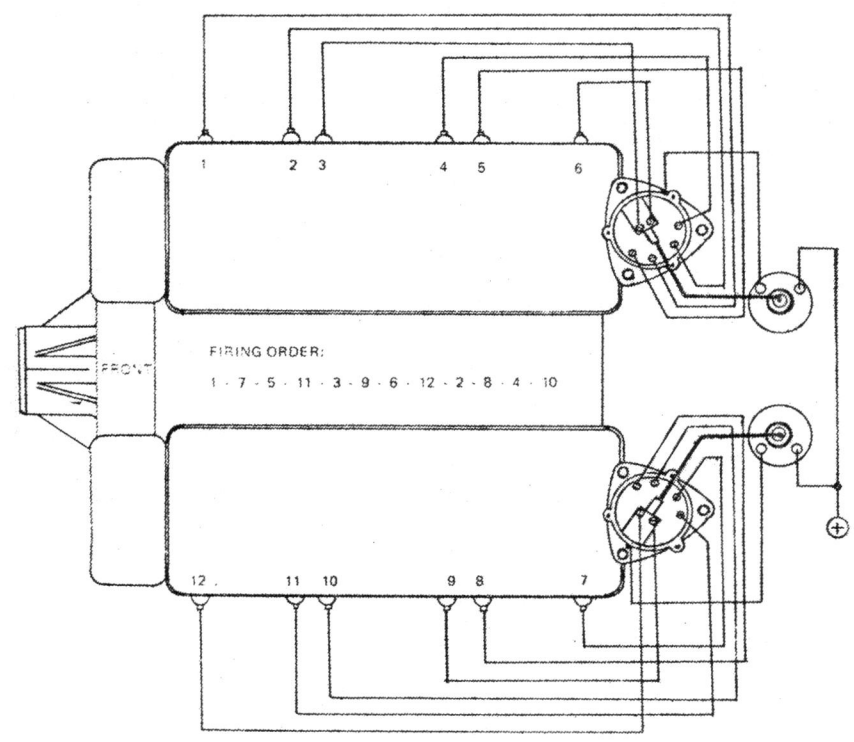

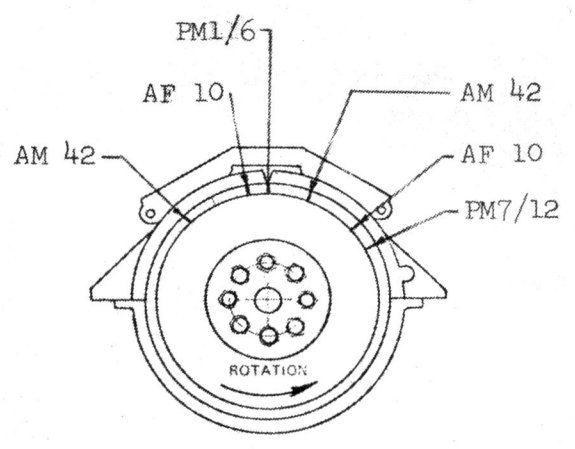

PM1/6 = Punto Morto; TDC for cylinder #1

PM7/12 = Punto Morto; TDC for cylinder #7

AF 10 = 10° Anticipo Fillo; 10° Fixed advance

AM 42 = 42° Anticipo Massimo; 42° Maximum advance

FLYWHEEL VIEWED FROM REAR (looking toward front of car)

SECTION II - ENGINE PART D - ENGINE COOLING SYSTEM

The purpose of the cooling system is to remove the excess heat from the engine – most of this heat resulting from the ignition system causing the combustion of the fuel mixture supplied by the carburetion system – and transfer this heat to another location where it can be dissipated. This is accomplished on a Ferrari by having a coolant mixture circulated through the engine and then to the radiator where air is forced through the passages, cooling the coolant mixture.

Some heat is necessary for efficient operation – that is why your Ferrari runs better after it is warmed up – but too much heat is disastrous. So it is essential that your cooling system operate efficiently.

This part of the Engine Section deals with such cooling system maintenance procedures as cold weather precautions and the use of antifreeze; flushing the cooling system; and information on radiator caps, thermostats, cooling fans, etc.

COOLING SYSTEM SPECIFICATIONS

	System Capacity	Thermostat Opens	Maximum Temp.	System Pressure	Fan(s) Activate/Deactivate	
250 GTE 2+2	11 lt	70°-77°C	90°-95°C		84°C	75°C
	11.6 qt	158°-165°F	190°-195°F	7 psi	183°F	167°F
275 GTS/GTB	12 lt	80°-85°C	110°C	.9 kg/sq cm	84°C	75°C
	12.7 qt	176°-185°F	230°F	13 psi	183°F	167°F
330 GT 2+2	14 lt	80°-85°C	95°-100°C		84°C	75°C
	14.8 qt	176°-185°F	203°-212°F	5 psi	183°F	167°F
330 GTC	14 lt	68°C*	115°C	.9 kg/sq cm	84°C	75°C
	14.8 qt	155°F*	239°F	13 psi	183°F	167°F
365 GT 2+2	14 lt	68°C*	115°C	.9 kg/sq cm	84°C	75°C
	14.8 qt	155°F*	239°F	13 psi	183°F	167°F
365 GTB/4	17.5 lt	83°C	115°C	.9 kg/sq cm	84°C	75°C
	18.5 qt	181°F	239°F	13 psi	183°F	167°F
DINO 246	17 lt	83°C	115°C	.9 kg/sq cm	84°C	75°C
	18 qt	181°F	239°F	13 psi	183°F	167°F

*NOTE: Cars intended for cold weather areas may be fitted with thermostats set to open at 78°C or 172°F.

COOLING SYSTEM MAINTENANCE

Proper maintenance of the Ferrari cooling system is essential for good vehicle performance.

EVERY 300 MILES:

> Check the level of the water in the radiator. Top up to ¾ in from cap seat with pure distilled water if required.

EVERY 3000 MILES:

> Check electric fan drive for operation.
> Check or set air gap of fan to .014 in.
> Check the belt tension. Tension should be 3/8 in deflection with 9 lb pressure on belt.

EVERY SIX MONTHS:

>Check all hoses for leaks or hardening.
>Drain and flush entire cooling system. It is recommended that this be timed to coincide with installing anti-freeze in the system.

COOLING SYSTEM MAINTENANCE

EVERY 12,000 MILES:

>Check water pump glands and ball bearings, and replace if leaky or noisy.
>Test radiator cap for relief pressure.
>Check fan armature brush and slip ring for wear.
>Replace the belts.

COLD WEATHER PRECAUTIONS

According to Dick Merritt, who supplied the basics of the following information in <u>The Prancing Horse</u>, no. III, there are three choices facing the Ferrari owner in cold weather: Drain the radiator and engine; add sufficient anti-freeze; or weld up the cracks some spring.

DRAINING

This supposedly simple operation has caused more grief than is often realized since turning the handy drain cock on the bottom of the radiator does not entirely drain the V-12 engine. Ferrari manuals may not always clarify this point, but the 250 GTE 2+2 Operating, Maintenance and Service Handbook makes pointed reference to the crankcase drain cock (see page 17 of the manual).

The block drains are brass hex-shaped plugs located on the lower side of the cylinder block, cleverly concealed below the exhaust pipes and devilishly inaccessible. Some early Colombo engines have only one plug, with either a passage in the block or a copper pipe connecting the two banks of cylinders so both drain completely. Later powerplants have a plug on each side, and both must be removed.

Two precautions concerning the block drains: One, the passage for the drain plug on the block may be jammed with rust particles. Be sure when draining to run a small piece of stiff wire in and out of the hole vigorously to dislodge any scale, etc. Two, on engines with the copper pipe connecting the cylinder banks, the pipe may be full of sediment, meaning that one bank can not be drained by any means. There is no way of insuring that the pipe is not blocked. It is located inside the clutch housing behind the flywheel, and removal is a monumental job. Whenever the engine is out of the car and dismantled, be sure to check this little item.

Since the Lampredi series engines do not have block drain plugs, but do have a very low-mounted water pump, it is likely that these do drain through the radiator. However, you still run the risk of water passages becoming plugged with scale, rust particles, and stop-leak compounds.

If you are determined to drain your car, fit the brass cylinder block drain plugs with small petcocks so the operation can be readily accomplished without wrenches. The plugs are usually quite stubborn about removal.

ANTI-FREEZE

Now it gets confusing. Again, there is a choice, and the battle lines are clearly drawn: Alcohol (methanol) based anti-freeze solutions versus ethylene glycol (Prestone, for example) based anti-freeze solutions.

Advocates of alcohol claim that it is relatively cheap and does not tend to seep into the crankcase and contaminate the oil. Even if it does, it is not likely to cause harm in small quantities and the sturdy twelves have been known to run for months in this condition. Those high on alcohol (excuse the pun) point to the fact that Ferraris are wet sleeve engines and therefore prone to seepage, so it is best not to take chances. They also insist that corrosion is not as severe as with the ethylene glycol year-round permanent solutions.

The ethylene glycol adherents are quick to point out that alcohol in any strength for really cold weather protection has a relatively low boiling point. This drives off considerable coolant mixture and the radiator must be constantly checked and topped up. To be safe you have to have an anti-freeze hydrometer and take periodic readings. With the permanent anti-freeze coolants this boiling dilemma is avoided.

The biggest problem with ethylene glycol is its reaction with oil. If you have a leaking head gasket, a cracked block or head, or any slight imperfection in the sealing of your cooling system – some people swear these compounds have a miraculous ability to seep through seals, gaskets, and castings where pure water will not pass – the ethylene glycol will pas into the oil and contaminate it. Glycol congeals when mixed with oil, and in doing so, plug oil filters, passages, etc. A white discoloration on the dipstick is the danger signal, and the most convenient check point is the oil filters. If your filter sludge looks like "curdled milk and molasses", you have trouble. Unless corrected by a thorough flushing of the lubrication system, the ultimate result will be a seized engine.

PURE WATER V. ANTI-FREEZE

The owner's manuals for Ferraris up through the 365 GT 2+2 and the Dino 246 recommended the use of pure water in the cooling system during warm weather, and Shell Anti-Freeze in freezing weather. Beginning with the 365 GTB/4 and the Dino 308, the factory recommends the use of an "anti-freeze mixture" year-round. No matter which type of coolant you use, change it at regular intervals. The additives in the so-called permanent anti-freeze solutions wear out long before the anti-freeze itself.

FLUSHING THE COOLING SYSTEM

The average person's idea of flushing the cooling system consists of opening the radiator drain cock, sticking a hose in the radiator filler, and letting the water flow until the discharge from the drain cock appears to be clear. However, this only flushes the radiator – the thermostat remains closed, blocking water circulation through the engine. Opening the engine block drain(s) will do nothing to alleviate this, as the engine water passages are still not being "flushed" to remove residue from old dirty coolant.

There are several methods of effectively flushing the engine. One is outlined in the 330 GT 2+2 Operating, Maintenance, and Service Handbook as follows:

1. Open all the drains and allow as much of the old coolant to drain out as possible.

2. Close all of the drains. Refill the system with a solution of three gallons of water and 11 oz of sodium carbonate.

3. Allow the engine to idle for at least 15 minutes – until the temperature is high enough to allow the thermostat to open and the solution to be circulated throughout the entire cooling system.

4. Drain completely.

5. Allow the engine to cool, then flush the system with running water, leaving the drain taps open.

6. Fill the system with water and allow the engine to idle for a few minutes.

7. Drain completely. Repeat the above steps until the draining water is clean.

8. Refill the system with the required coolant.

Another method, and one that is now commercially available as a kit, is to introduce a flow of clean water through the heater supply hose. This forces water through the cooling system counter to normal circulation bypassing the closed thermostat.

INSTALLING ANTI-FREEZE

When using ethylene glycol anti-freeze, such as Prestone brand, the following percentages of anti-freeze/water will give the protection indicated:

25%/75%	10°F
30%/70%	4°F
35%/65%	-3°F
40%/60%	-12°F
45%/55%	-22°F
50%/50%	-34°F
55%/45%	-48°F
60%/40%	-62°F

RADIATOR CAPS

The radiator cap fitted on all late model Ferraris is identified in the factory spare parts catalogs as an FIM 252841 cap – this applies to all V-12 engine cars from the 275 GTS/GTB through the 330, 275 GT/4 Cam, 365 GT/2 Cam and 365 GT/4 Cam series. This is alleged to be a standard Dole no. R-9 cap.

The same range of cars are also fitted with expansion tanks, and the same sources identify the cap for this tank as an FIM 252733/A.

THERMOSTATS

The thermostats fitted to Ferrari V-12 engined cars present a much more confusing picture.
The 250 GTE has a thermostat fitted in the top radiator hose – see page 51 of the Operating, Maintenance and

Service handbook.

The early 275 GTS/GTB is listed as having a DTV 35 P35.F34 thermostat. After December 31, 1965 this was changed for a D35-54 thermostat. Both thermostats were fitted in the radiator header tank at the upper outlet.

The 275 GTB/4 has the thermostat in the same location, but it is designated as a BOA 14640.

The 330 GT 2+2 mounted the thermostat in the engine water inlet. It was designated a P35 DTV35 F54 in the spare parts catalog for the Mark I version, and just P35 F54 in the spare parts catalog for the later version.

The 330 GTC also mounted the thermostat in the engine water inlet, and used a BOA 14640 designation.

The 365 GT 2+2 and early 365 GTB/4 spare parts catalogs show thermostat type JUCKER x1.001.83.100, again mounted in the engine water inlet. Later 365 GTB/4s, after serial no. 13801, were fitted with a BEHR X2.038.79.100 thermostat.

The Dole DVN-I H 185° thermostat is supposed to be an acceptable substitute for the 330 GT 2+2 thermostat, and by extension, also the 275 GTS/GTB.

RADIATOR REPAIR/REFINISHING

If your radiator (or heater core, for that matter) is damaged, trust the repair only to a reputable shop – check around for one in your area.

When refinishing a radiator, use a _thin_ coat of enamel paint. Too much paint may affect the thermal transfer characteristics.

THERMOSTATICALLY CONTROLLED COOLING FAN(S)

All V-12 Ferraris from the 250 GTE 2+2 on have been fitted with thermostatically controlled cooling fan(s).

On the earlier types (250 GT, 330 GT 2+2 Mk. I) the fan is powered by a crankshaft-driven belt. It is fitted with an electronic clutch which should engage when the water temperature reaches approximately 183°F, and disengages when the water temperature falls below 167°F. Periodically check this clutch for proper operation, and adjust the air gap to 0.14 in my means of the three 7 mm bolts on the front hub.

The fan can also be permanently engaged – if, for instance, the thermoswitch which controls it fails – by tightening these same 7 mm bolts.

Later Ferraris were fitted with electronically powered cooling fan(s). They were also equipped with thermoswitches which were designed to activate the electric fan(s) when the water temperature reaches approximately 183°F, and break the electric circuit with the water temperature falls below 167°F.

Ferraris that are normally fitted with air conditioning – such as the 365 GT 2+2 and the 365 GTB/4 – are also fitted with two electric cooling fans. When the air conditioning is switched on, the right hand fan is also activated regardless of the water temperature. The left hand fan continues to operate in the normal manner, not activating until the water temperature reaches 183°F. When the air conditioning is not on, both fans operate in the normal manner.

Periodically check the electric fan(s) to be sure they are properly activating.
The electric cooling fan and relay used on the 275 and 330 were manufactured by Lucas of England and are the same as those used on the Jaguar XK-E. These should be available from a Jaguar dealer or an auto parts dealer who handles Lucas components. FAF Motorcars stocks all Lucas items that are available for Ferraris.

If you are having problems with your electric fan motors, try installing anew set of brushes before you go shopping for a new motor. Brush sets are available, again, from your favorite source of Lucas parts.

WATER PUMP CARBON SEAL

If water is leaking through the water pump drain hole you probably need a new carbon seal. Before installing this seal, check the steel plate on the back of the brass impeller and make sure it is perfectly smooth, i.e., does not have any grooves worn in it. If it does, you can use some valve lapping compound and a piece of plate glass to grind it smooth.

SECTION II - ENGINE PART E - ENGINE LUBRICATION SYSTEM

As your Ferrari engine operates – if all of the preceding systems are functioning correctly – a lot of different bits and pieces are in constant and intermittent motion, rubbing, scraping, pushing, pulling, etc. against other bits and pieces. This causes friction, heat, and wear. To keep these within reasonable limits is the purpose of the lubrication system.

All moving parts in the car, not just those in the engine, require lubrication. But in this section we will deal only with engine lubrication. The lubrication of other components will be taken up in later sections. Working with the lubrication of any component is an easy way to get dirty, and for this reason many fastidious Ferrari owners disdain such operations and entrust them to someone else. But it is also one of the easiest and most essential operations to perform yourself. The dirt will wash off.

This part of the Engine Section deals with the lubricants for the engine, and covers such topics as oil level, recommended types of oil, and information on oil filters.

ENGINE OIL RECOMMENDATIONS

For the factory recommendations on oil types to be used, see page 14 of this manual.

CASTOR OIL

Francisco Laboratories, 3015 Glendale Boulevard, Los Angeles, CA 90039, has been producing castor oil for automotive use for many years. This manufacturer is well known as the leading producer of racing fuels and oils for all types of internal combustion engines.

Although castor oil is expensive in comparison to petroleum oil, many advantages are claimed. Francisco Laboratories content that tests have proven the highly superior lubricating qualities of castor oil – as little as one-fifth the cylinder wear experienced with petroleum oil – and total lack of dilution by engine fuel.

In the past, designers and manufacturers of racing and aircraft engines have recommended that castor oil be used, but that it be removed and flushed from the engine within 24 hours after use. With Francisco Laboratories' oil, however, this is not necessary because of the degumming process.

A few Ferrari owners have been using Francisco castor oil in their Ferraris for years for a much more practical reason – it drastically reduces the amount of exhaust smoke.

Be sure to drain your petroleum oil thoroughly and change your oil filters if you decide to try a change to castor oil.

MULTI-GRADE OIL

Multi-grade oil may not provide proper lubrication at high temperatures and high rpms. One Ferrari owner ran his own tests, Porsche reported on the shortcomings of such oil, and a representative of an oil company explained that multi-grade oils may not provide the right viscosity under severe loads. If you subject your Ferrari engine to such extremes, you may want to stick with a single weight oil – SAE 40 in the Summer and SAE 30 in the Winter.

OIL LEVEL

Unlike the customs on American cars, late model Ferraris should _not_ be driven with the oil level indicating below the MAX mark on the dipstick. The MIN position indicates a several quart deficiency which can, on hard braking, acceleration, or high speed cruising, result in a partial loss of oil pressure.

On Ferraris equipped with a dry sump system, the level of the oil in the oil reservoir must be checked _immediately_ after shutting down the engine. Oil will flow back into the engine from the reservoir if the car is allowed to stand for a few minutes. If you check the oil level after this has happened, you will get a false low reading. Adding oil based on such a reading would result in overfilling. The excess oil will be blown out the breather holes and throughout the engine compartment.

If you check the oil in your dry sump car after it has been standing overnight, the level should read halfway between MIN and MAX.

Finally, be sure to periodically clean the dry-sump drain-back on your Ferrari so equipped.

OIL LINES FOR DRY SUMP CARS

Reinforced lines, as used for dry sump Ferrari engines, were supplied the factory by a French manufacturer:
>Superflexit
>M. Boberewski
>Rue des Minimes
>Courbevoie, 92 France

OIL SUMP CAPACITY

The oil sump capacity on the 275 GTB/4 is 17 quarts. However, merely draining the engine only produces approximately 12 or 13 quarts of dirty oil. In order to complete drain the sump, it is necessary to remove the cover plate. Failure to do this results in approximately four quarts of dirty oil being left in the engine with each oil change.

OIL FILTERS

Early 250 GT Series engines (128 B, C, D) used a Fram canister type oil filter, mounted on side of engine compartment, which used a replaceable filter cartridge, C-30.

Later 250 GT Series engines (128 E, F, 168), and early 275 GT/2 Cam and 330 GT Series engines (to about 1966) used a bypass oil filter system, with the filters mounted on each side of the front of the engine. This system used two different oil filters – on Fram PB 50 bypass type oil filter, and one Fram PH 3. The PH 3 is no longer available, but the Fram PH 2815 makes a very suitable replacement.

Later 275 GT/2 Cam and 330 GT Series engines (after 1965), the 275 GT/4 Cam Series engine, and all 365 Series engines use a full flow oil filter system, with the bypass built into the mounting plate. The filters are mounted close together at the front of the engine. This system uses two Fram PH 2804 filters.

The Dino 206, 246 and 308 Series engine also use the Fram PH 2804 filter, but only one.

There are many possible substitutions for these recommended filters. The owner contemplating such a substitution should be aware of the following possible trouble points in making substitutions:

1. Burst Strength. The recommended Fram oil filters have a minimum burst strength of 500 psi, except the PB 50, which is a bypass filter. The Fram PH 8 and its equivalents, which fit and are often used on Ferraris, bursts at about 200 psi, hence they can rupture under cold weather starting conditions. It is a terrifying experience to see your oil pressure gauge suddenly drop to zero, and then have to face a long job to clean up the oil in your engine compartment.

2. Internal Pressure Relief Valve To Allow Bypassing A Clogged Filter. The Fram PH 8 and its equivalents have a bypass valve which operates at about 7 to 9 psi, which is much too low for the high pressure Ferrari oil pump. Most of the time the oil will be bypassing the filter. The PH 2815

bypasses at 28 psi.

3. Anti-Drain Back Valve. Since Ferrari oil filters are inverted compared to normal practice, the recommended filters have a valve which keeps oil in the filter so it can get to the engine faster when the engine is started. The valve also keeps oil from running all over the engine when the filter is removed.

4. Effective Filtration. The paper used in single element filters is only as good as the quality control of the manufacturer. Some inexpensive, lower grade filters have paper of wildly varying porosity. The PB 50, because it is a bypass filter, traps particles as small as .0002 in, while the other filters trap particles as small as .0006 in.

So, before employing a substitute filter on your Ferrari, check it out thoroughly on the above points. If it fails to meet the specifications of the recommended filters, you are taking a chance. Yes, the substitute filters may be cheaper – but have you priced a complete engine rebuild lately?

SECTION II - ENGINE PART F - ENGINE EXHAUST SYSTEM

The common conception of the exhaust system is that it is a sort of sewer pipe whose main function is to conduct the wastes that are created by the combustion of the fuel mixture to the rear of the car. Along the way mufflers have been placed to keep the noise of the engine within reasonable limits.

The exhaust system is more than just a necessary nuisance. A properly designed and functioning exhaust system is essential to good performance – and keeping the Fuzz off your back.

This part of the Engine Section deals with the exhaust headers, exhaust mufflers, and exhaust tail pipes.

EXHAUST HEADERS

Part of a concourse condition engine compartment is the appearance of the exhaust headers. To improve their looks, remove them from the engine and have them sandblasted clean. Then spray them with VHT or similar high quality high temperature paint. Then reinstall the headers, using new gaskets.

The headers may be sprayed on the engine, although the results are not as nice and you run the risk of spraying something else as well. If you spray them on the engine, clean them first with a stiff wire brush.
After painting the headers, they will smoke the first time they get hot. This is just the paint baking on, and is normal.

EXHAUST SYSTEMS

The current manufacturer of Ferrari exhaust systems is ANSA, and replacement systems – complete, muffler section, or tailpipe section, are available in the U.S.A. for all cars from the 250 GT through the Daytona and Dino 246. Before you rush down to your local ANSA retailer, however, be aware of the following:

250 GT

The system manufactured by ANSA as a replacement for the 250 GT may not fit your car. This Ferrari was manufactured over a period of years, and apparently used various configurations of exhaust systems. One purchaser of the ANSA system for his 250 GT SWB Berlinetta – a car which was originally fitted with an Abarth system – found that extensive modifications were needed to make it fit his car.

250 GT BERLINETTA LUSSO

Again, a car that was originally fitted with an Abarth exhaust system in many cases, and one which the ANSA replacement may not fit. However, one owner of a Lusso has found that the 250 GTE system made by ANSA can be fairly easily modified to fit the Lusso, provided you can weld or can find a welder willing to do the job.

FAF Motorcars, who are a retailer of ANSA exhaust systems for Ferrari's can supply information sheets on the necessary modifications. All you have to do is ask – you don't eve have to order the system before requesting the information.

365 GTB/4 DAYTONA

There are three systems manufactured for the Daytona – two for European versions and one for the American version. The European versions and the American versions are not interchangeable. The European versions have four inlet pipes, while the American has only two. The tailpipes have different mounting brackets. So check your car before ordering a new system to be sure which type you have.

STAINLESS STEEL EXHAUST SYSTEMS

Both the American version Daytona exhaust system and the 365 GTC/4 exhaust system are manufactured partially from stainless steel. Consequently, they are quite expensive.

If you want a complete stainless steel exhaust system, one which should never cause a problem due to rust or corrosion, they are available, usually custom built, from various specialty firms in England. But be advised that we have checked into this and while their work comes highly recommended, their prices are quite high, and the time it takes to acquire one of these jewels is rather lengthy.

EXHAUST SYSTEM LEAKS

For minor leaks in the exhaust system – something that must be corrected before tuning and carburetors – try the muffler cement type of patching. A tube should cost less than a $1.00 at your local auto parts supply dealer, and will temporarily solve the problem.

EXHAUST HANGERS

It has been suggested that a replacement for broken or rotted exhaust system hangers for Ferraris was available at Triumph automobile dealers. The TR-6 strap, part no. 138961, costing about $.50 each, was supposed to be of about the right dimensions.

We know of at least one Ferrari owner who tried this, and found there were several shortcomings. One was that the straps from Triumph were all rubber, whereas the Ferrari straps have metal ends. The triumph straps, consequently, wore out quite rapidly. Also, this same owner found that while the dimensions were close, they were not really close enough to make the Triumph hangers a really suitable substitute.

SECTION III - CLUTCH AND TRANSMISSION

Now that you have finished Section II and have the heart of your Ferrari, its engine, in perfect running order, it is time to take the next step and transmit the power of the engine to the rear wheels. The first step in this process is the subject of this Section III – Clutch and Transmission.

The clutch is, on all manual transmission cars, a weak link. It was designed as such – it was designed to wear out, and how fast or slow it accomplishes this is dependent upon the driver. On powerful cars, and the Ferrari is such a car, its limits are even more critical, and its proper care and maintenance more necessary for satisfactory performance.

The transmission, or gearbox, is not designed to wear out. But it is often abused. And without the gearbox, the power of the engine cannot be transmitted to the rear wheels. So it too must be properly maintained and cared for.

CLUTCH SPECIFICATIONS

The 250 GT and 275 GT/2 Cam engines through 1966 were fitted with clutch latest and discs made by a German company, Fichtel & Sachs AG, and were Type HB225Sph.

Fichtel & Sachs AG also made the clutches, Type HB250Sph 1882.88.101 that were used on the early 330 GT 2+2, the 400 SA, the 250 GTO and the 500 SF.

From the later 330 GT 2+2 and 275 GT/2 Cam, through the 275 GTB/4, 330 GTC and 330 GTS, and all 365 series Ferraris, the clutches have been supplied by Borg & Beck. Over the years a confusing variety of numbers have been used in reference to these clutches. The Ferrari Factory Service Bulletins state that the latest Borg & Beck clutches, as used on the 365 GTB/4 and 365 GTC/4, are interchangeable with all earlier models that used Borg & Beck clutches.

The Dino 246 uses a clutch assembly supplied by a French company, Verto, which is a division of Ferodo.

SUBSTITUTIONS

For the earlier cars – those fitted with Fichtel and Sachs AG clutches – it may be possible to find some interchangeable parts at your local Mercedes-Benz dealer, since M-B also uses this brand of clutch. For example, the 250 GT series Ferrari uses the same disc (part no. 1861.084.002) and pressure plate as the Mercedes 300s.

There are many other possible substitutions that will fit. But beware!! Some of these may be unsafe, while others may lack the durability to last under the demands of a Ferrari. For instance, we know that Fichtel & Sachs' HB20Sph 1882.188.102 pressure plate assembly will work on a Ferrari that should be fitted with an HB250Sph 1882.188.101 assembly, but it is _not_ a satisfactory nor safe replacement. We have also heard that clutch discs from Austin-Healey 3000s will work, but wear out in only a few thousand miles.

It is recommended that a _qualified_ expert be consulted before any substitutions are attempted.

CLUTCH MAINTENANCE

EVERY 500 MILES: Check free play.

EVERY 1000 MILES: Adjust linkage and pedal free play.

EVERY 2000 MILES: Lubricate linkage

EVERY 5000 MILES: Bleed clutch hydraulic system if hydraulic-actuated type clutch system is fitted to your Ferrari.

EVERY 10000 MILES: Check disc and pressure plate for damage or wear.

EVERY 15000 MILES: Rebuild hydraulic cylinder if hydraulic-actuated type clutch system is fitted to your Ferrari.

EVERY 20000 MILES: Replace clutch disc. Recondition flywheel and pressure plate. Replace throwout bearing.

CRANKSHAFT AND TRANSMISSION OIL SEALS

When replacing the clutch on Ferraris with front-mounted transmissions, check for any indication of oil leaks in the bellhousing. If there is evidence of such leakage, it is advisable to replace the crankshaft rear seal and the transmission front seal.

CLUTCH MASTER AND SLAVE CYLINDERS – 330 GT SERIES

Clutch master cylinders have two seals. FAG repair kit RK25602 contains two seals, one of which will replace the leaking primary seal.

FAG repair kit RK19606 contains two seals, one of which will replace the seal in your slave cylinder.

FIAT slave cylinder part no. 4188216 is identical to the 330 GT slave cylinder, complete with rubber boot.

FIAT part no. 996020 is the Ferrari replacement for the 330 GT clutch hydraulic system hose.

GEARBOX AND CLUTCH REMOVAL

These instructions are applicable to 250 GT, 275 GT and 330 GT series Ferraris fitted with front (in unit with engine) mounted transmissions.

GEARBOX REMOVAL

1. Remove both front seats.

2. Remove carpets and gearshift knob.

3. Unbolt transmission tunnel from firewall and floor.

4. Lift the tunnel out, carefully clearing the shift lever.

5. Unbolt the rear drive shaft flange at the universal joint.

    NOTE: On some Ferraris it may be easier to disconnect the front universal joint.

6. Remove the drive line from the transmission. About 3 in separation is sufficient to clear the rearward motion of the box.

7. Unbolt the transmission mounting(s) located directly under the tail stock. Some gearboxes, and those with overdrive units, will have additional mounts 5to remove.

8. Drain the transmission fluid on gearboxes fitted with overdrive. This is optional on straight gear boxes, and is intended to reduce the total weight.

9. Remove all bellhousing bolts.

10. Remove the clutch linkage and speedometer cable.

11. Disconnect any electrical connections, such as backup lamp and overdrive control wires.

12. Place the shift lever in neutral.

13. Place a small jack under the rear of the engine.

14. NOTE: The gearbox is to be removed through the inside of the car.

15. Rock the gearbox from side to side to be sure that all attachments have been removed.

16. Place wooden blocks under the front of the gearbox so it will not drop to the floor when disengaged from the engine.

17. With the help of an assistant, slide the gearbox rearward away from the engine. A slight rocking motion may help free it up.

18. Carefully slide the spline pilot shaft all the way out of the engine. The gearbox should be completely free of the vehicle.

19. Lift the gearbox out of the vehicle and place on wooden supports. Do not drop the gearbox on hard surfaces or you might crack the housings. To prevent damage to the splines, cover them with rags.

CLUTCH REMOVAL

1. With the gearbox removed, the clutch assembly is completely accessible at the rear of the engine.

2. Using a six-point socket to prevent stripping the bolt heads, unbolt the six pressure plate securing bolts. Loosen each bolt only a few turns at a time, so that the pressure plate pushes away from the flywheel evenly without binding.

3. The pressure plate and the disc are now free to be removed. Slip the throwout bearing off the shaft.

4. Inspect the flywheel and pressure plate for damage or warpage. Have a qualified expert repair or replace all damaged materials

5. Inspect the pilot bearing in the rear of the crankshaft. Replace or regrease as required.

GEARBOX DISSASSEMBLY AND EXAMINTION

With the gearbox out of the vehicle, it can be disassembled and inspected for wear and damage. Procedures for this operation – if you feel you can handle it, it is not a chore for beginners – can be found in English in the 330 GT 2+2 Workshop Manual.

GEARBOX AND CLUTCH INSTALLATION

CLUTCH INSTALLATION

1. If the flywheel has been removed, remount it to the rear of the crankshaft aligning the locating pin carefully.

2. Install all of the original flywheel bolts (DO NOT substitute bolts of a lower grade) and keeper straps. Torque flywheel bolts to 35 ft lb. Recheck all bolts. Peen keeper straps over.

   NOTE: If excessive material was cut from the pressure plate to correct defects, the flywheel bolts may have to be ground down.

3. Using a clutch alignment shaft (most auto supply stores have adjustable sets), place the disc and pressure plate against the flywheel.

4. Install all pressure plate bolts. Slowly tighten each a few turns at a time, so that the pressure plate closes evenly without binding, until tight. Torque to 30 ft lb. Recheck all torques again, and remove alignment tool.

GEARBOX INSTALLATION

1. With the gear level in neutral, place the gearbox in the vehicle, supported by a wooden support, and aligned with the engine.

2. Lift the gearbox into the rear of the engine. A small amount of side motion must be applied to seat the spline in the clutch.

3. Slide the gearbox all the way up to the engine so that the studs protrude through the bellhousing.

4. Install the bellhousing nuts and lock washers, and torque then to 20 ft lb.

5. Connect all electrical and speedometer connections to the gearbox.

6. Connect the clutch linkage, and adjust to allow correct free play.

7. Bolt the transmission mounts down, and apply safety wire where holes are provided.

8. Remove jack from under engine.

9. Connect the drive shaft. Torque and wire all bolts.

10. Fill the gearbox (and overdrive if fitted) with fresh lubricant.

11. Replace the transmission tunnel, gearshift knob, carpets and seats.

12. Check the clutch and gearbox for property operation. Readjust the clutch linkage if necessary.

TRANSMISSION PRECAUTIONS WHEN TOWING

When towing the car in neutral, the transmission oil pump does not operate. Therefore, if towing for long distances, it is a good practice to engage the transmission occasionally for a few hundred yards, thus enabling the oil pump to operate and lubricate the gear cluster bushings of the mainshaft.

> NOTE: If the engine is damaged and cannot be turned, take care to not engage the clutch while the transmission is in gear.

REPAIR OF SHIFT LEVER BUSHING

If your shift lever has a lot of play in it, it probably has a cracked bushing on the lower end. Ferrari has supplied bushings in two different materials. Early bushings are caramel colored and are not noted for longevity. Later bushings are black, have a split in them, and are of a much harder composition.

The same size bushing has been used on Ferraris from the late 350 GT series through the 365 GTB/4 and Dino series.

Replacing the busing can be accomplished by following these directions, applicable to Ferraris with front mounted transmissions.

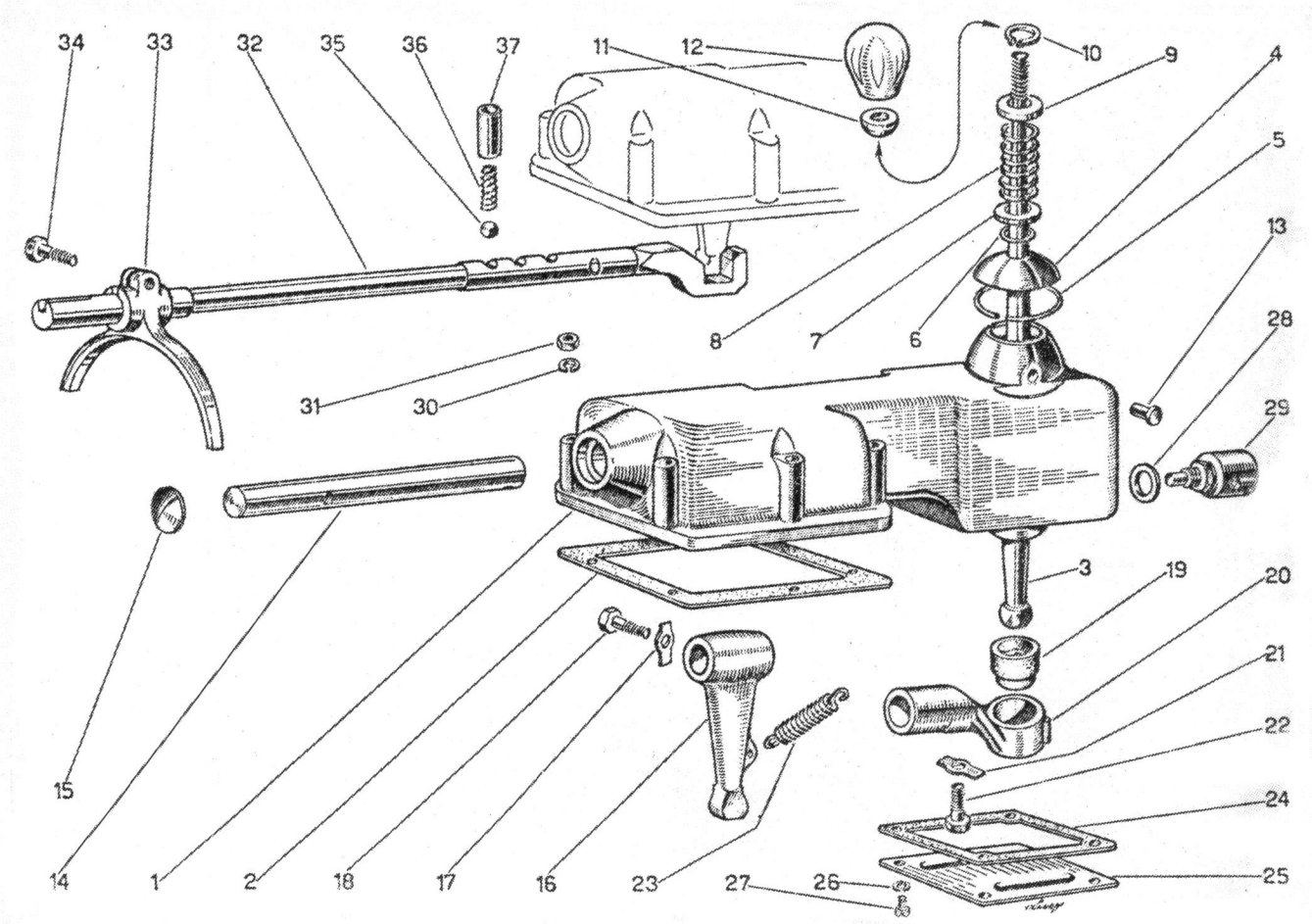

NOTE: Numbers in parenthesis ( ) refer to above illustration.

1. Remove gear shift knob (12) and jam nut (11).

2. Remove transmission tunnel cover.

3. Remove housing nuts (31) and lock washers (30).

4. Lift lever housing (1) up and out of gearbox. Lever must be in neutral.

5. Remove screws (27) and washers (26). Lift cover plate (25) off.

6. Remove bolt (22) and tab (21).

7. Slide shaft (14) forward and pull socket (20) off of shaft.

8. Pull broken or cracked bushing (19) from shaft (3).

9. check spring (23). Replace I broken

10. Grease ball of lever (3) with bearing grease.

11. Force new bushing (19) on ball of lever (3).

12. Push shaft (14) forward. Slip socket (20) onto shaft.

13. Push socket (20) over bushing (19).

14. Align shaft (14) and socket (20) bolt holes.

15. Install bolt (220 and tab (21), bending tab up after tightening.

16. Grease all moving components well, and install cover plate (25) with screws (27) and washers (26).

17. With shift lever (3) in neutral position, install in gearbox.

18. Torque case nuts (31) with washers (30) to approximately 5 ft lb.

250 GTE 2+2 OVERDRIVE UNIT

A weak point on the 250 GTE 2+2 is the English manufactured overdrive unit. To avoid trouble:

1. Be sure the transmission/overdrive oil is thoroughly warmed before driving fast or hard.

2. Avoid full-throttle shifts.

3. Periodically clean the overdrive oil pump screen and magnet. These are accessible by removing the large round brass plug at the base of the unit. See page 58 of the 250 GET Operating, Maintenance and Service Handbook.

TRANSAXLES

On Ferraris equipped with a transaxle, the drain plug for the unit is also the filter unit for the pump, thereby making it impossible to fit a magnetic drain plug. In addition, the drain plug is located on the side of the case, about ¼ in above the floor of the transaxle. This makes it impossible for all the oil to drain out.

One owner recommends the periodic "sweeping" of the floor of the casing with a magnet parts retrieving tool in order to pick up any metal particles.

TRANSMISSION LUBRICANTS

The factory recommendations for gearbox lubricants can be found on page 15 of this manual.

Shell Spirax is their standard product line, and should be available at all gas stations.

The EP (extreme pressure) designation has been changed to HD (heavy duty), and the greases are not formulated to work in limited slip differentials.

Shell Spirax HD is available in 80, 90 and 140 weights.

It is important that you use only Shell Spirax HD or equivalent lubricants. Some companies manufacture lubricants with the EP designation that also contain active or passive held sulfur and/or chlorine and/or lead.

SECTION IV – DRIVE SHAFT

After the clutch and transmission, the next step in getting power to the rear wheels is the drive shaft. We don't have much in the way of tuning tips and maintenance techniques for the drive shaft, just the following:

UNIVERSAL JOINTS

When rebuilding the universal joints on late model Ferraris, the damaged or decomposed cork grease seals should be replaced. These hard to find seals can be replaced with standard "O" rings. A Parker Seal Company part no. 2-209 works very well. They measure 11/16 in inside diameter, 15/16 in outside diameter, 1/8 in wide, and each universal joint requires four (4) of them. They are available in most cities from jobbers. If not available in your area, write for their catalog and distributor listing at::

    Parker Seal Company
    10567 Jefferson Boulevard
    Culver City, CA 90230

SECTION V – DIFFERENTIAL AND REAR AXLE

Again, not much in the way of tuning tips and maintenance techniques for the next step in the drive train, the differential and real axle.

DIFFERENTIAL LUBRICANTS

Shell Dentax 250, which was the recommended lubricant for some Ferrari rear axles (see page 15 of this manual) is now virtually impossible to obtain. Shell Spirax HD 140, or any good quality SAE 140 gear lube, is a perfectly good alternative as far as lubrication properties are concerned although its use may cause some increase in differential noise.

365 GT 2+2

The differential lubricant recommended for this type was Shell S 1747 A. The Ferrari Factory Serviizio Assistenza Tecnica advises, however, that from Serial No. 13067 this type, fitted with self-locking differential with molybdenum sprayed blades, should use Shell Spirax HD 80 in the differential.

This does not apply to the 365 GTB/4, which should still be supplied with Shell S 1747 A lubricant for the differential.

LIMITED-SLIP DIFFERENTIAL CLATTER

In limited-slip differentials that clatter, use General Motors Anti-Spin Rear End additive, part no. 1050428.

DRAINING REAR AXLE LUBRICANTS

When draining the lubricant from the differential, be sure the oil is warm.

SECTION VI - REAR SUSPENSION
and
SECTION VII - FRONT SUSPENSION

For reasons of logistics, we have combined these two sections into one. This was quite easy to do, since the only information we have on either the rear or the front suspension is the alignment specifications.

SUSPENSION ALIGNMENT SPECIFICATION

Specifications for the rear suspension alignment will be found on the following pages.

Specifications for the front suspension alignment will be found on the following pages.

For both sets of specifications, the following conditions must apply:

1. All dimensions are to be taken at static load with two passengers, full fuel tank, spark wheel, and tool kit.

2. Values must be within tolerances.

3. Values must be the same for right and left side.

    NOTE: The specifications on the following tables may not match those given in the individual vehicle's owner's handbooks. These specifications were taken from a technical service bulletin published by Ferrari Servizio Assistenza Tecnica.

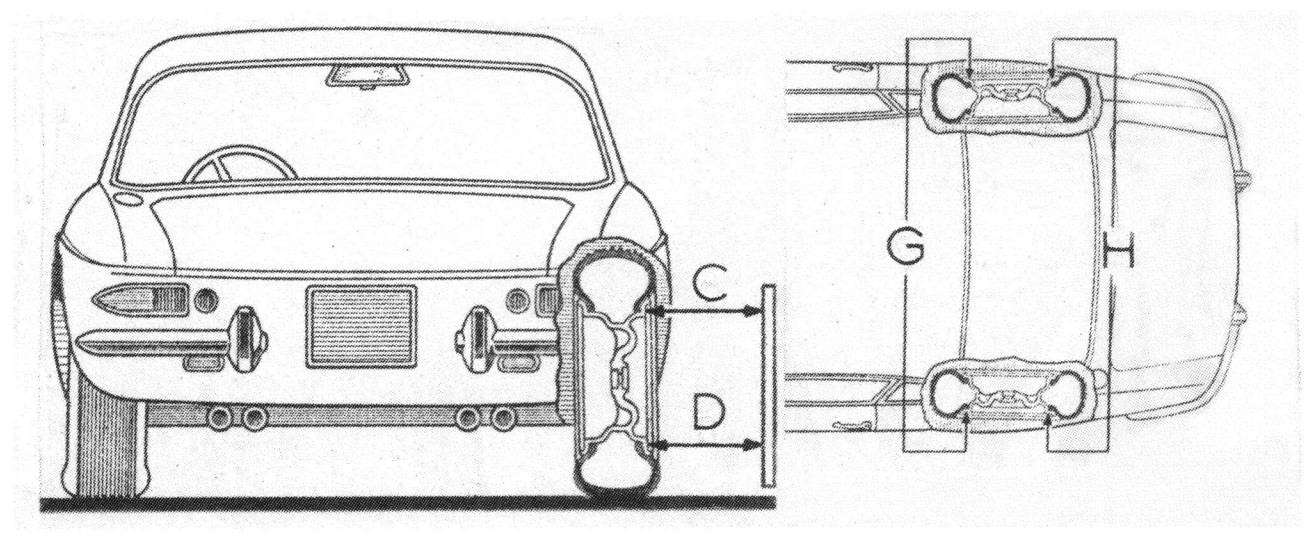

REAR SUSPENSION ALIGHMENT SPECIFICATIONS

Model	Camber	Toe-in/Toe-out
250 GT Lusso	C=D+0.00mm (min) =+0°00' C=D+0.00mm (Max) =+0°00'	G=H (Min) G=H (Max)
250 GT Calif 250 GTE 2+2 330 GT 2+2	C=D+0.00mm (min) =+0°00' C=D+0.00mm (Max) =+0°00'	G=H (Min) G=H (Max)
275 GTB/FTS 275 GTB/4	C=D+5.17mm (min) =+0°50' C=D+7.76mm (Max) =+1°15'	G=H-4mm (Min) G=H-6mm (Max)
330 GTC/GTS	C=D+5.17mm (min) =+0°50' C=D+7.76mm (Max) =+1°15'	G=H-5mm (Min) G=H-5mm (Max)
365 GT 2+2	C=D+7.10mm (min) =+1°05' C=D+10.53mm (Max)=+1°35'	G=H (Min) G=H (Max)
365 GTC/GTS	C=D+10.34mm (min) =+1°40' C=D+12.41mm (Max)=+2°00'	G=H-5mm (Min) G=H-5mm (Max)
365 GTB/4	C=D+15.00mm (min) =+2°15' C=D+16.50mm (Max)=+2°30'	G=H-2mm (Min) G=H-3mm (Max)
365 GTC/4 365 GT4/2+2	C=D+10.00mm (min) =+1°30' C=D+12.00mm (Max)=+1°50'	G=H (Min) G=H (Max)
365 GT4/BB	C=D+10.10mm (min) =+1°30' C=D+12.30mm (Max)=+1°50'	G=H-2mm (Min) G=H-4mm (Max)

Model	Camber	Toe-in/Toe-out
Dino 206 GT	C=D+7.75mm (min) =+1°15'	G=H (Min)
Dino 246 GT	C=D+9.31mm (Max) =+1°30'	G=H-3mm (Max)
Dino 308 GT4	C=D+8.60mm (min) =+1°20'	G=H-2mm (Min)
	C=D+10.75mm (Max) =+1°40'	G=H-4mm (Max)

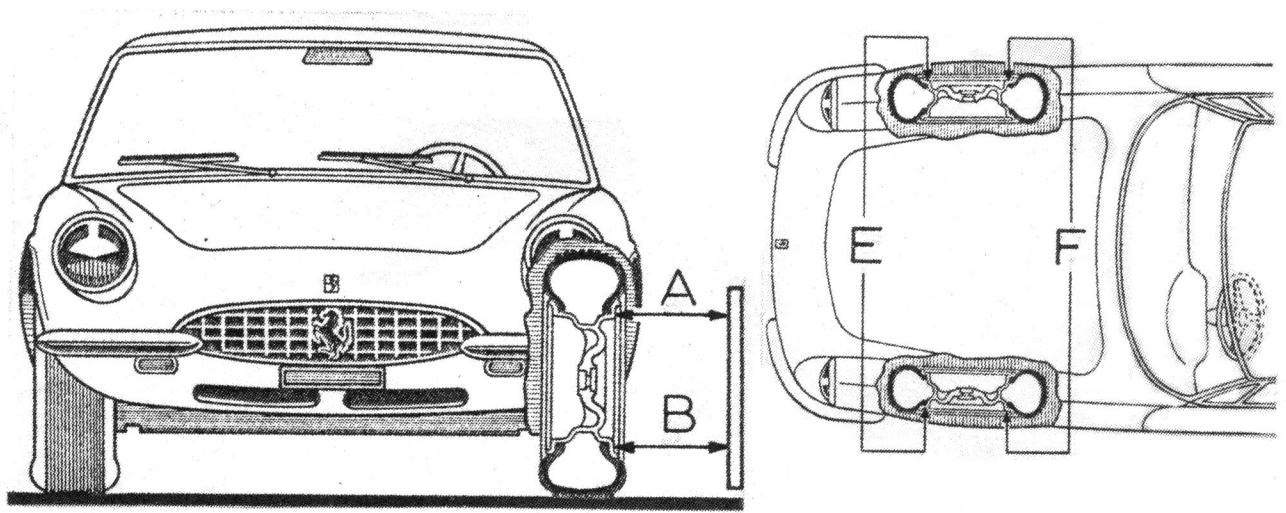

FRONT SUSPENSION ALIGNMENT SPECIFICATIONS

Model	Camber	Toe-in/Toe-out	Caster	Kingpin
250 GT Lusso	B=A+5.54mm (min) =+0°50' B=A+8.31mm (Max) =+1°15'	E=F (Min) E=F-2-3mm (Max)	2°30'	9°
250 GT Calif 250 GTE 2+2 330 GT 2+2	B=A+5.54mm (min) =+0°50' B=A+9.42mm (Max) =+1°25'	E=F (Min) E=F+2mm (Max)	2°30'	9°
275 GTB/FTS 275 GTB/4	A=B+0.00mm (min) =+0°50' A=B+2.06mm (Max) =+0°20'	E=F-4mm (Min) E=F-5mm (Max)	2°30'	9°
330 GTC/GTS	A=B+0.00mm (min) =+0°00' A=B+2.06mm (Max) =+0°20'	E=F-4mm (Min) E=F-5mm (Max)	2°18'15"	9°
365 GT 2+2	B=A+3.32mm (min) =+0°30' B=A+6.64mm (Max) =+1°00'	E=F (Min) E=F+3mm (Max)	2°30'	9°
365 GTC/GTS	A=B+0.00mm (min) =+0°00' A=B+2.06mm (Max) =+0°20'	E=F-4mm (Min) E=F-5mm (Max)	2°18'15"	9°

Model	Camber		Toe-in/Toe-out	Caster	Kingpin
365 GTB/4	A=B+5.50mm (min) A=B+7.50mm (Max)	=+0°50' =+1°10'	E=F-2mm (Min) E=F-3mm (Max)	1°30'	9°
365 GTC/4 365 GT4/2+2	A=B+5.00mm (min) A=B+7.00mm (Max)	=+0°40' =+1°00'	E=F-2mm (Min) E=F-3mm (Max)	3°	9°
365 GT4/BB	A=B+3.40mm (min) A=B+6.00mm (Max)	=+0°30' =+0°50'	E=F-1mm (Min) E=F-3mm (Max)	4°	9°
Dino 206 GT Dino 246 GT	A=B+1.55mm (min) A=B+3.10mm (Max)	=+0°15' =+0°30'	E=F (Min) E=F-3mm (Max)	3°40'-4°	9°30'
Dino 308 GT4	A=B+1.00mm (min) A=B+3.25mm (Max)	=+0°10' =+0°30'	E=F-1mm (Min) E=F-3mm (Max)	4°	9°30'

SECTION VIII - SHOCK ABSORBERS

HOUDAILLE SHOCK ABSORBERS

Up through the early 250 GT series Ferraris, the standard shock absorber fitted was the Houdaille lever-action type. One source for rebuilding these shock absorbers is:

>Earl Gruber
>11777 LaBella Avenue
>Sunnyvale, CA 94087

KONI SHOCK ABSORBERS

Beginning with the later 250 GT series Ferraris, Koni adjustable shock absorbers have been standard equipment on all Ferraris.

While the manufacturer of KONI shock absorbers publishes a list of the recommended shock absorbers for each Ferrari type, be aware of the fact that there is a lot of vibration on some Ferrari models. Before purchasing replacement shock absorbers, be sure to check those already on your Ferrari to be sure you are getting the correct replacement.

Ferrari Type	Year	Front	Rear
250 GT to chassis no. 2417	1960	82H-1191	82H-1200
250 GT from chassis no. 2417	1960/61	82H-1191	82H-1205
250 GT and GTE	1961/62	82H-1216	82H-1217
250 GT SWB Spyder California	All	82H-1191	82H-1205
250 GT SWB Berlinetta and GTO	All	82R-1238	82R-1239
250 GT, GTE and Lusso	1962/1964	82H-1216	82R-1322
250 GTE, 330 GT America and 2+2	1964/65	82H-1321	82R-1322
275 GTB and GTS (to Feb. 1966)	1965/66	82N-1349	82N-1350
275 GTB and GTS (after Feb. 1966)	All	82N-1451	82N-1452
330 and 365 GTC and GTS	All	82N-1451	82N-1452

365GT2+2	All	82H-1604	82N-1573
365 GT 2+2 Self-leveling units	All	—-	7100-1004
365 GTB/4 and GTS/4	All	82T-1633	82P-1634
365 GTC/4	All	82T-1750	82N-1751
365 GTC/4 Self-leveling units	All	—-	7100-1012
365 GT4/2+2	All	82T-1824	82N-1825
365 GT4/2+2 Self-leveling units	All	—-	7100-1012
365 GT4/BB (Four required at rear)	All	82T-1833	82T-1834
DINO 206 and 246 GT and GTS	All	82P-1579	82N-1603SP2
DINO 308 GT4	All	82P-1830	82P-1831

INSTALLING KONI SHOCK ABSORBERS

KONI shock absorbers are specially manufactured for each type of vehicle. Therefore, first check to be sure the correct types of Koni shock absorbers are available to be fitted.

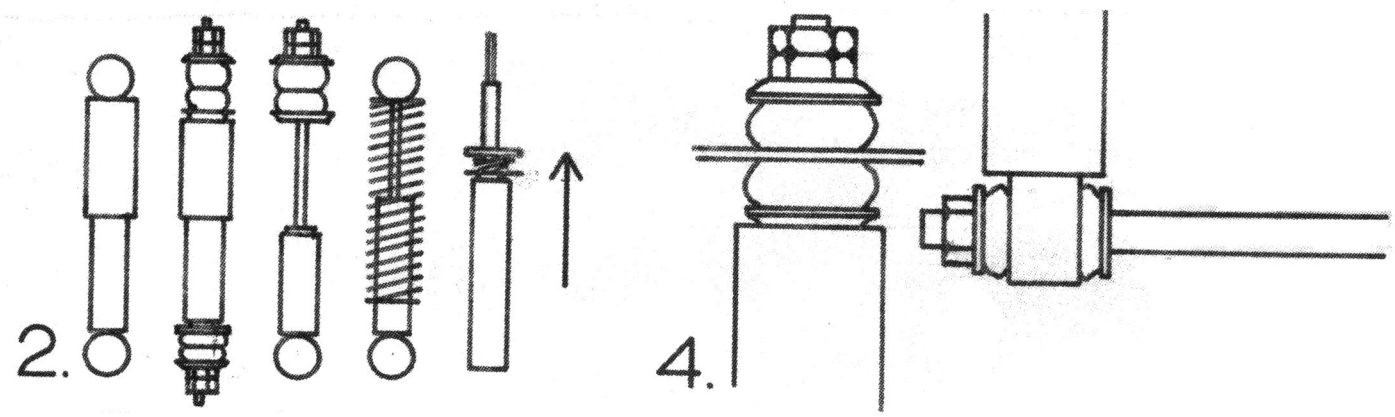

1. Due to friction in the glands, it may be difficult to extend the shock absorber when installing. After installation, the shock absorbers will free-up after the first 60 to 70 miles (100 km).

2. Fit shock absorbers straight from the box with piston rod upwards. The arrow on the damper tube must be in the upward position (see diagram above).

3. Fit rubber bushings, nuts, etc. in the same sequence as they were on the attachments when un packing.

4. Tighten home the fixing nuts until they reach a metal stop, either bushing or collar. When there is no metal bushing or collar, stop after rubber bushings bulge slightly due to compression (see above).

5. Be sure that the shock absorbers do not foul chassis or body parts during either the bump or rebound movements of the suspension.

ADJUSTING KONI SHOCK ABSORBERS

If, only after thousands of miles, the damping effect of the KONI shock absorbers requires adjustment, this can be done as follows:

NOTE: Always adjust shock absorbers in pairs – two front or two rear – and always adjust both shocks for the same amount.

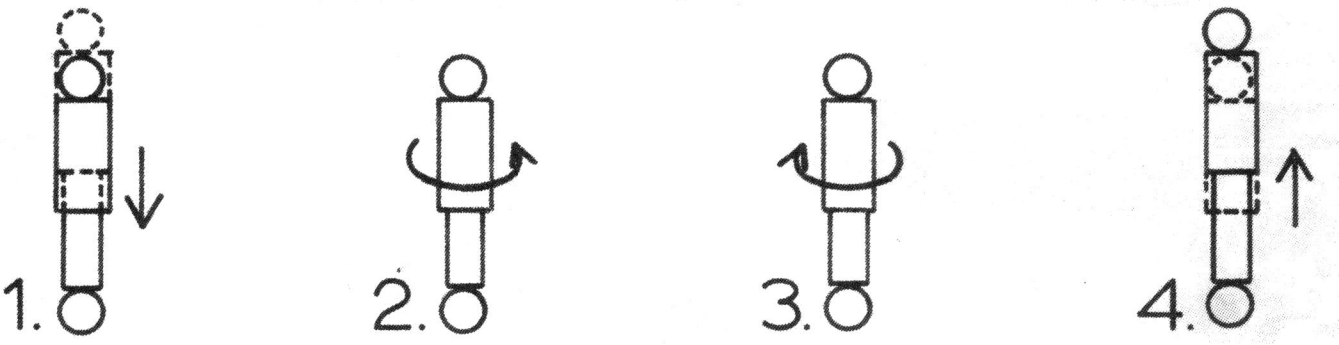

1. Remove the shock absorber from the vehicle, place the lower end in a vice, and fully compress the shock absorber.

2. Turn the top to the left without using force until the teeth of the adjuster nut can be felt engaging with the recesses of the footvalve assembly. Continue to turn gently to the left until no further motion is possible. Do not force additional motion or damage will occur.

3. While maintaining a slight closing pressure, make two half turns (a total of 360° or rotation) to the right. The total range of adjustment is four to five half turns.

4. Pull damper out for about one inch, taking care not to turn any further, to allow the teeth of the adjuster nut to disengage. The shock absorber can now be fitted to the vehicle.

REBUILDING KONI SHOCK ABSORBERS

One source for rebuilding or modifying KONI shock absorbers is:

McAfee-McKenzie Enterprises, Inc.
2806 Burbank Boulevard
Burbank, CA 91505
213-8458525

SECTION IX - STEERING

STEERING SYSTEM MAINTENANCE

On all late model Ferraris, the steering linkage does not require periodic lubrication. If you are experiencing trouble with your car's steering, first check the following conditions:

1. All steering and suspension components should be free of damage and operating property.

2. Front and rear wheels should be correctly balanced and set for camber and toe-in.

3. Tires should be correct pressures and not excessively worn.

4. Shock absorbers are of correct type and operating efficiently.

ROUTINE MAINTENANCE

EVERY 3000 MILES: On cars equipped with hydraulic steering, check the condition and operation of the pump belt.

EVERY 6000 MILES: Check the level of the oil in the steering box, and replenish if necessary. See page 15 of this manual for recommended lubricants.

> NOTE: On cars equipped with hydraulic steering, the level of the oil in the tank should be checked every 600 miles.

> Check the free play of the ball joints.

> Check the free play of the worm and roller, and adjust if necessary.

TIE-ROD ENDS

Tie-rod ends used on old Alfa-Romeos are interchangeable with those used on the Ferrari 250 GT.

SECTION X - BRAKES

ROUTINE MAINTENANCE

Frequency	Operation
Every day	Check pedal pressure before driving at speed.
Every 500 Miles	Check brake fluid level and replenish if needed.
Every 1000 Miles	Check parking brake and adjust if necessary.
Every 1500 Miles	Bleed entire brake system.
Every 5000 Miles	Change all brake fluid. Clean disc rotors using #400 emery to remove any surface rust or glaze.
Every 7500 Miles	Inspect all rubber brake hoses and replace as necessary
Every 10,000 Miles	Replace all disc pads.
Every 20,000 Miles	Rebuild disc actuating cylinders and master cylinder.
Every 40,000 Miles	Rebuild rotor discs.
Every 50,000 Miles	Replace all flexible brake hoses.

BRAKE FLUID

The brake fluid you use in your Ferrari should be disc type and exceed SAE Standards J1703 and Type 70R3 requirements. Never mix different types of fluids. Acceptable fluids include:
        ATE Tipo H
        Castrol GT LMA
        Dunlop Racing Brake Fluid
        Kelsey-Hayes Kelstar Disc Brake Fluid No. 7999
        Shell Donax-B SAE 70R3

Maintain brake fluid reservoir at least ¼ full at all times, but never more than ¼ in from the top. Never reuse old brake fluid. When replenishing, always use new fluid, and when changing fluid, always use new brake fluid from unsealed cans.

When bleeding the brake fluid system, start from the boosters on top and work down to each wheel. Allow at least 60 seconds for the pedal to return.

PREVENTING BRAKE SYSTEM PROBLEMS

In addition to the routine maintenance outlined on the previous page, there are other measures that the Ferrari owner should take to prevent brake problems.

The most common problem with Ferrari disc brakes is the tendency of the brake pads to freeze to the caliper body. Ferraris are particularly susceptible to this problem, which plagues all disc brake systems, because Ferrari owners are often meticulous creatures who take great pains to preserving their automobiles.

The basic cause of the problem is inactivity. Cars which are not driven in the winter often suffer this problem. Periods of inactivity allow the corrosive elements to work. This is especially true if the car is not put up until after it has had some exposure to early winter driving. Proximity to a body of salt water also causes problems.

The solution to the problem requires preventative maintenance, as follows:

1. Thoroughly wash the exposed areas after driving in salt spray.

2. Remove the pads and thoroughly clean the caliper body every six months. Coat the sliding surfaces (not the braking surface) of the pad with anti-seize compound before reinstalling. Work the piston back and forth in the caliper bore with the appropriate tool before replacing the pad.

3. Thoroughly flush the brake system at regular intervals in order to remove any moisture absorbed by the brake fluid. Moisture-laden brake fluid is a major cause of caliper bore corrosion.

BRAKE SYSTEM SPARE PARTS

BRAKE HOSES FOR EARLY FERRARIS

Brand new brake hoses for very early Ferraris are available from:
         Don Wasserman
         1127 Irving Street
         San Francisco, CA 94122
         415-731-9100

These have big ends, are 17-1/2 in long, and have copper sealing rings. Don also has new brake shoe return springs available for Ferraris up to the 250 MM.

SEALS FOR EARLY MASTER CYLINDERS

Replacement seals for the early tandem-type master cylinders of 1 in diameter can be found in repair kits for the Volkswagen Bus. Three such kits are:
- VW kit no. 211-698-411
- ATE kit no. 3.0470-2425.2
- FAG kit no. RK 2527

Each kit contains only one seal that can be used, so it will be necessary to buy three kits to get enough seals to rebuild the unit.

STEEL BRAKE FLUID RESERVOIRS

Some early model Ferraris used steel brake fluid reservoirs. These containers are prone to rust if not kept full. If this has happened to yours, try replacing the old reservoir with a new transparent plastic one. Volkswagen has a complete selection of dual and single compartment brake fluid reservoirs.

To install the VW part, the steel tubing that connects to the old reservoir must be cut. Use a good grade copper tubing cutter and remove about 6 in from the fitting end just below the reservoir. Find a good quality neoprene fuel line of about ¼ in inside diameter that fits tight over the tubing, and use two mini-hose clamps to fasten the neoprene line between the old steel tubing and the bottom of the VW fluid reservoir.

It may be necessary to modify the new reservoir's mounting hardware – this is left to your individual ingenuity. The brake lines usually do not require bleeding after making this change if they were not pumped during the operation

DUNLOP DISC BRAKES

On later Ferraris using Dunlop disc brakes, brake pads, hoses, and miscellaneous parts can be ordered through Joseph Lucas of North America, Ltd. They have offices in many large cities. Another brake part source is your neighborhood Jaguar dealer. The Mark IX and XK-E shared some common parts with Ferraris. J.C. Whitney/ Warshawsky & Co. carries Jaguar pads that are about equal to the original 250 and 330 parts for <u>normal</u> use only. As with any substitute parts, always compare the originals with the substitutes. If any question arises, consult a qualified expert on the subject.

AKRON/DUNLOP/GIRLING/ATE BRAKE PARTS

Spare parts for Ferrari brake systems, from the early Akron drum type through the latest ATE disc type, are available from FAF Motorcars. This includes hoses, pipes, rebuild kits, cylinders, discs, pads, etc.

DUNLOP SERIES II CALIPER

USED ON:

All 250

All 275

All 330 GT 2+2

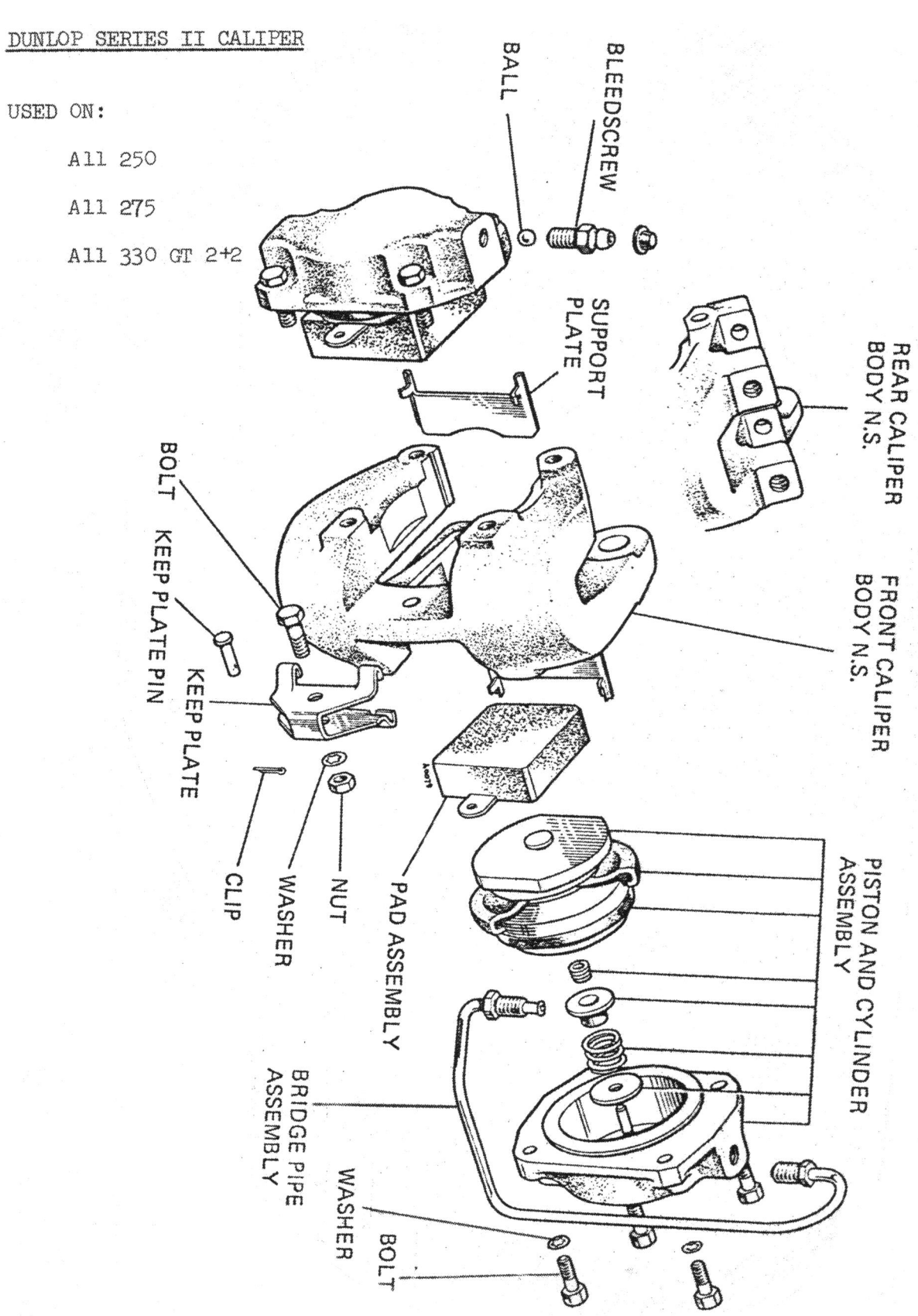

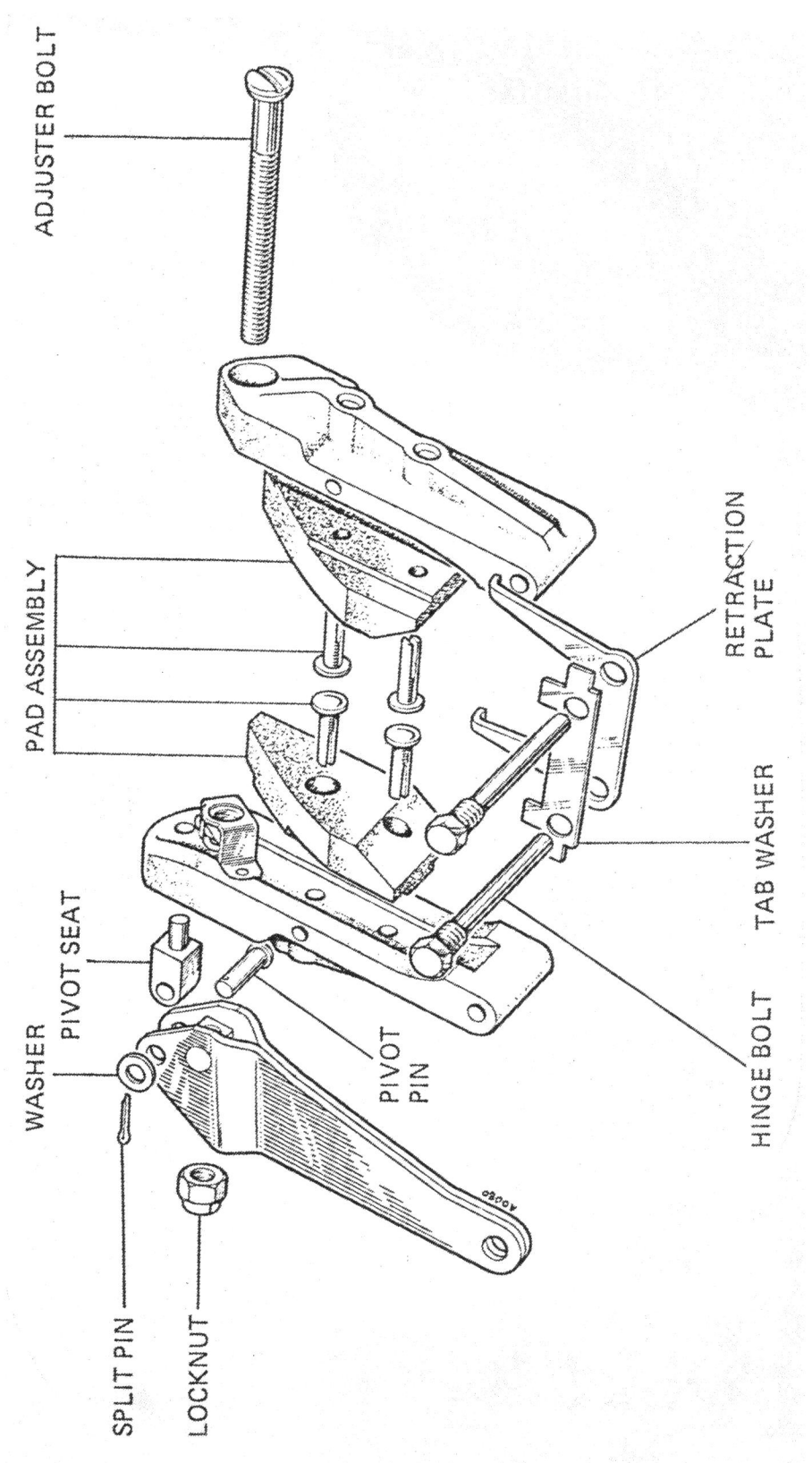

MANUALLY ADJUSTED HANDBRAKE

ter 330 GT 2+2

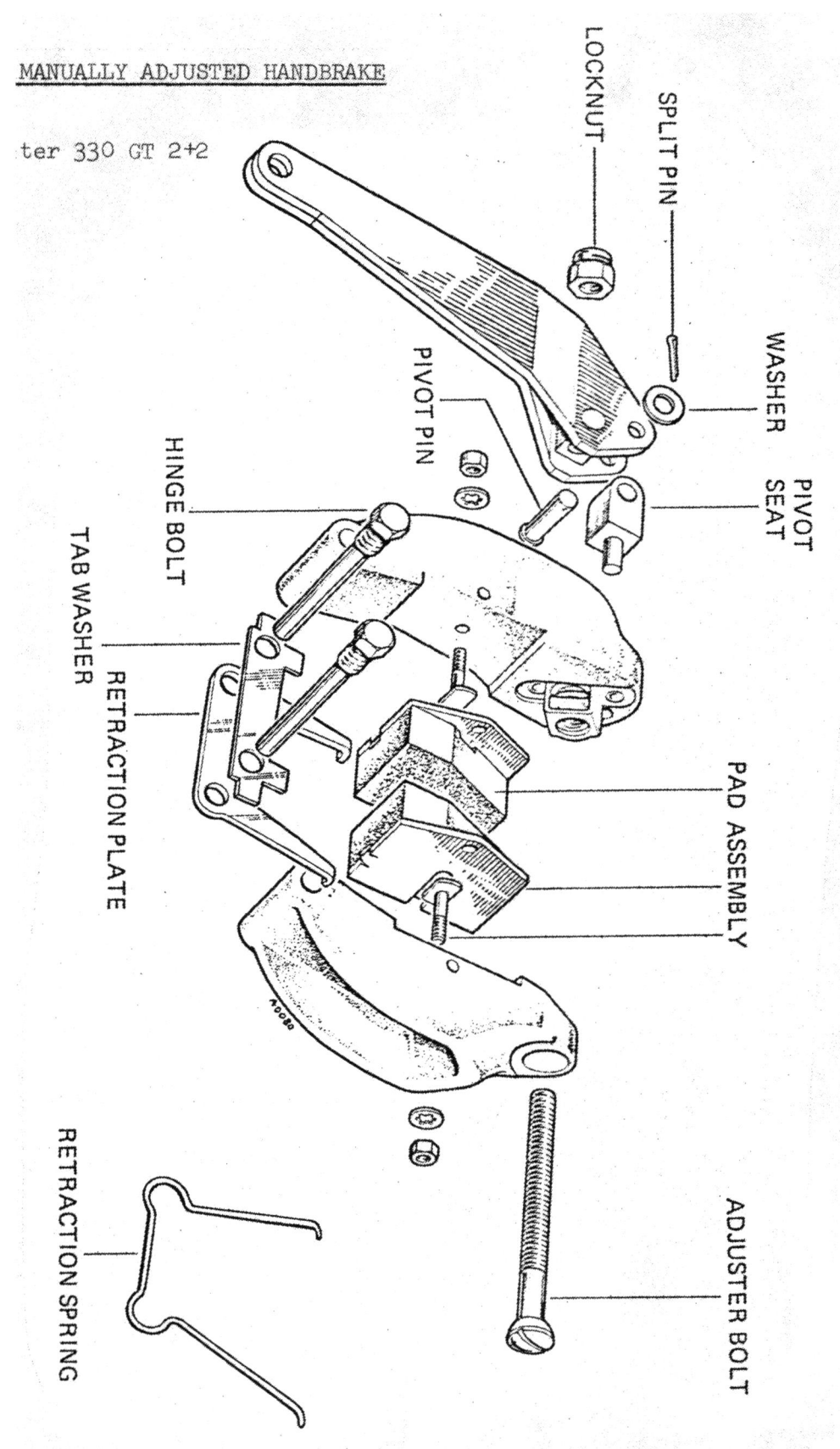

DISC BRAKE PAD AND ROTOR SPECIFICATIONS

The following information comes from Ferrari Circulare Tecnica No. 110/3, dated January 22, 1973

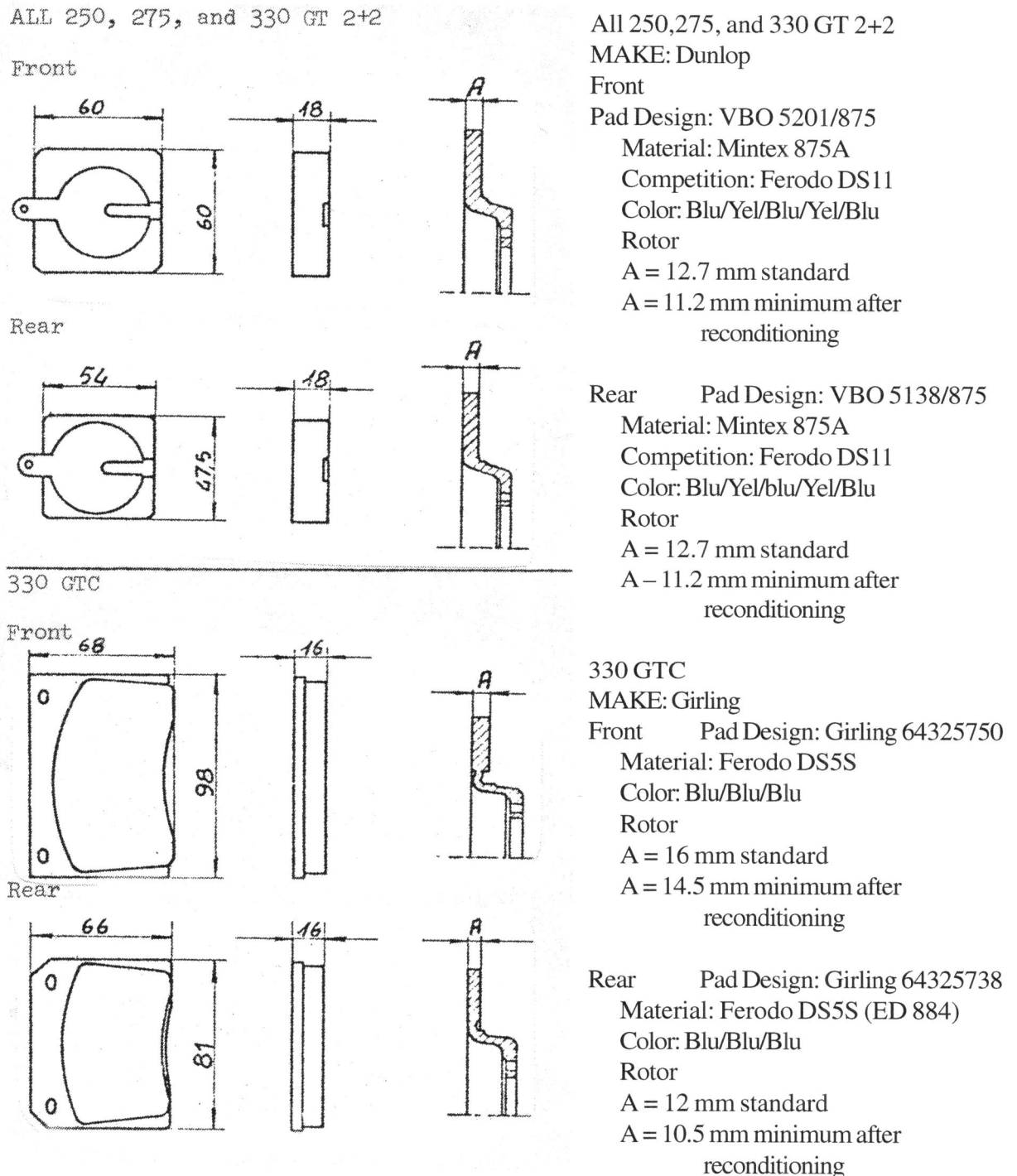

All 250, 275, and 330 GT 2+2
MAKE: Dunlop
Front
Pad Design: VBO 5201/875
    Material: Mintex 875A
    Competition: Ferodo DS11
    Color: Blu/Yel/Blu/Yel/Blu
    Rotor
    A = 12.7 mm standard
    A = 11.2 mm minimum after
        reconditioning

Rear   Pad Design: VBO 5138/875
    Material: Mintex 875A
    Competition: Ferodo DS11
    Color: Blu/Yel/blu/Yel/Blu
    Rotor
    A = 12.7 mm standard
    A – 11.2 mm minimum after
        reconditioning

330 GTC
MAKE: Girling
Front   Pad Design: Girling 64325750
    Material: Ferodo DS5S
    Color: Blu/Blu/Blu
    Rotor
    A = 16 mm standard
    A = 14.5 mm minimum after
        reconditioning

Rear   Pad Design: Girling 64325738
    Material: Ferodo DS5S (ED 884)
    Color: Blu/Blu/Blu
    Rotor
    A = 12 mm standard
    A = 10.5 mm minimum after
        reconditioning

NOTE: Dunlop was absorbed by Girling in the mid-1960s, and all Dunlop VBO numbers were changed to Girling 8-digit numbers.

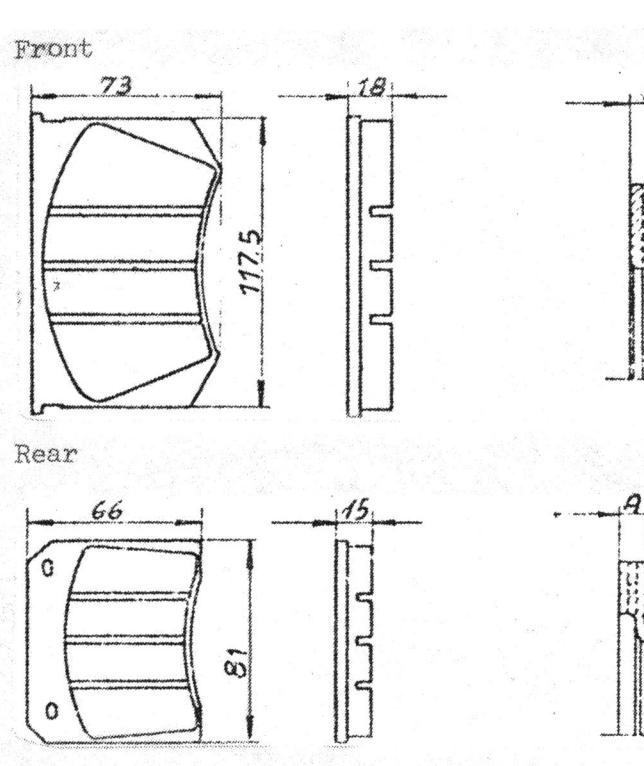

365 GT 2+2   MAKE: Girling
Front Pad Design: Girling 64320574
       Material: Ferodo FG2426F
       Color: Blu/Blu/Whi/Whi
       Alternate Design: Girling 64325738
       Material: Abex 254 GF
       Rotor
       A = 32 mm standard
       A = 30 mm minimum after
           reconditioning

Rear   Pad Design: Girling 64326119
       Material: Ferodo FG2426F
       Color: Blu/Blu/Whi/Whi
       Alternative Design: Girling
           64325839
       Rotor
       A = 21 mm standard
       A = 19 mm minimum after
           reconditioning

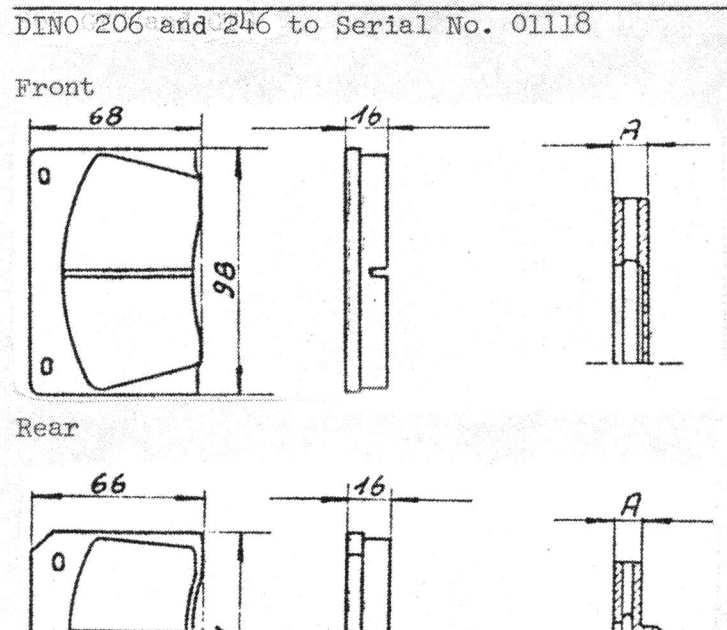

DINO 206 and 246 to Serial No. 01118
MAKE: Girling
Front Pad Design: Girling 64326120
       FIAT 1.65012/114 BS 100
       Material: Don 206
       Color: Yel/Red/Yel
       Rotor
       A = 26 mm standard
       A = 23 mm minimum after
           reconditioning

Rear   Pad Design: Girling 64326119
       FIAT 1.65212/114 BS 100
       Material: Don 206
       Color: Yel/Red/Yel
       Rotor
       A = 18 mm standard
       A = 16 mm minimum after
           reconditioning

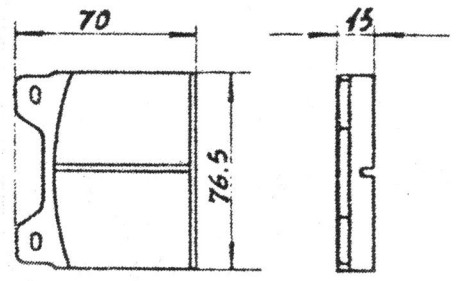
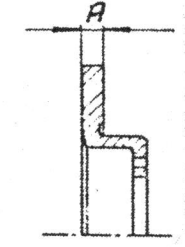

365 GTC and GTS
MAKE: ATE
Front Pad Design: ATE 13.8107/5419.2
    Material: Textar V1431Gff
    Color: Grn/Yel/Grn/Yel/Grn
    Rotor
    A = 16 mm standard
    A = 14.5 mm minimum after
        reconditioning

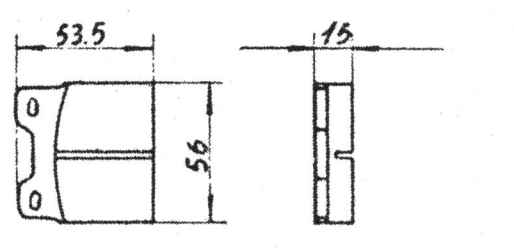
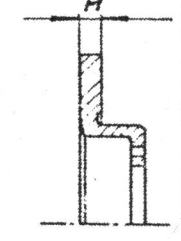

Rear Pad design: ATE 13.8107/3516.2
    Material: Textar V1431GFF
    Color: Grn/Yel/Grn/Yel/Grn
    Rotor
    A = 9.5 mm standard
    A – 8 mm minimum after
        reconditioning

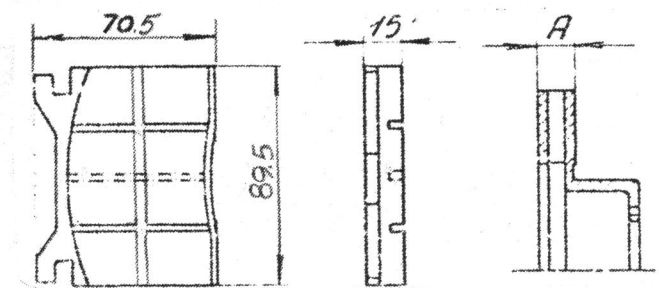

365 GTB/4, Early Versions
MAKE: ATE
Front Pad design: ATE 13.8107/9015.2
    Material: Textar T252GF
    Color: Grn/Grn/Grn/Whi/Whi
    Rotor
    A = 32 mm standard
    A = 30 mm minimum after
        reconditioning

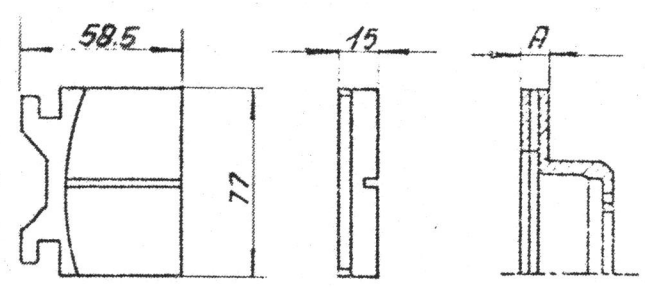

Rear Pad Design: ATE 13.8107/7704.2
    Material: Textar T252GF
    Color: Grn/Grn/Grn/Whi/Whi
    Rotor
    A = 22 mm standard
    A = 20 mm minimum after
        reconditioning

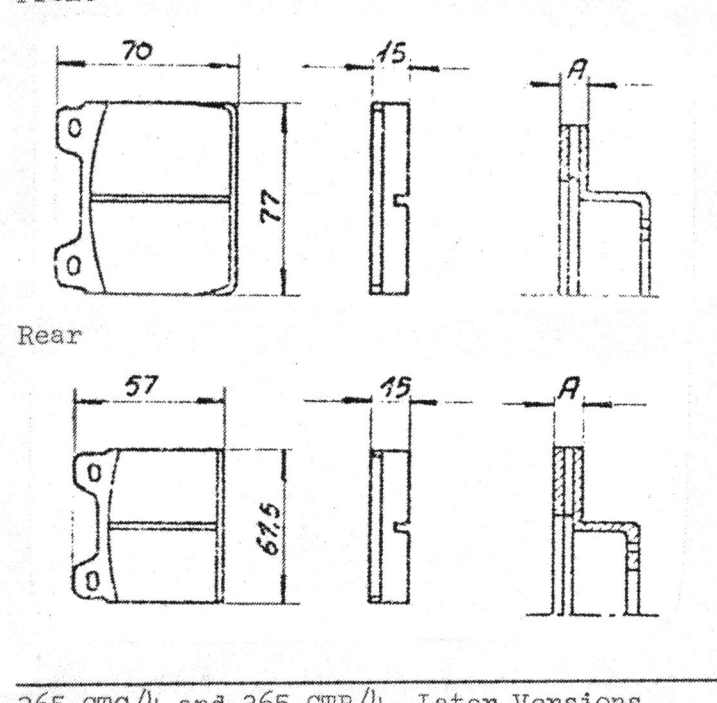

DINO 246 after Serial No. 01118
MAKE: ATE
Front Pad Design: ATE 13.8107/5418.2
  Material: Textar 1431FF
  Color: Grn/Whi/Grn Rotor
  A = 22 mm standard
  A = 20 mm minimum after reconditioning

Rear Pad Design: ATE 13.8107/4211.2 (right)
  Pad Design: ATE 13.8107/4210.2 (left)
  Material: Textar 1431FF
  Color: Grn/Whi/Grn Rotor
  A = 20 mm standard
  A = 18 mm minimum after reconditioning

365 GTC/4 and 365 GTB/4, Later Versions
MAKE: ATE
Front Pad Design: ATE 13.8107/9019.2
  Material: Ferodo I/D 330
  Color: Blu/Whi/Whi/Whi/Blu Rotor
  A = 32 mm standard
  A = 30 mm minimum after reconditioning

Rear Pad Design: ATE 13.8107/7702.2
  Material: Ferodo I/D 330
  Color: Blu/Whi/Whi/Whi/Blu Rotor
  A = 22 mm standard
  A = 20 mm minimum after reconditioning

BRAKE PAD COEFFICIENT OF FRICTION

A uniform identification code designating the coefficient of friction of the pad is now stamped on almost all disc brake pads sold in this county.

The first letter of the two letter code designates the normal friction coefficient, and the second letter designates the hot friction coefficient.

Code Letter	Coefficient of Friction
C	Not over 0.15
D	Over 0.15 but not over 0.25
E	Over 0.25 but not over 0.35
F	Over 0.35 but not over 0.45
G	Over 0.45 but not over 0.55
H	Over 0.55
Z	Unclassified

Example: A lining having a normal friction coefficient of 0.29 and a hot coefficient of friction of 0.40 would be coded "EF."

The appropriate code designation is supposed to be marked on an external noncontacting surface in letters not less than 0.125 in in height.

BRAKE SYSTEM REPAIR

BENDIX BOOSTER UNITS

Many Ferraris with early disc brake systems used a dual or two single Bendix booster units. Your local Bendix distributor or service agency can usually provide service on these units.

VACUUM BOOSTER LINE

On Ferraris with disc brakes there is a vacuum line from the booster to the intake manifold. If this line develops a leak it will affect the low-speed operation of the brakes – not much will happen when the brakes are applied. You will not notice it as much at high speed, and even at low speed it may be an on-again-off-again occurrence. A leak in this line also affects whichever carburetor it is nearest. Check this line and, if necessary, replace it with a Gates vacuum line of the same inside diameter. In fact, since the original equipment line is apparently prone to early failure, it is a good idea to go ahead and replace it anyway and avoid a future problem.

CUT BRAKE LINES

On the 365 GTB/4 a problem has been noted concerning the left rear flexible brake line. The culprit is the sheet metal splash shield which protects the fuel pumps. This shield forms part of the lower inner wheel well and will chafe against the brake line. It is a simple matter to remove the left rear wheel to see if this is occurring on your car. If it is, a simple reshaping of the shield will solve the problem. Be sure your reshaping still allows plenty of clearance to the inside of the rear tire.

A similar problem has occurred on some 330 GT 2+2 Ferraris. Here the culprit is a flexible steel cable which is attached to both sides of the rear axle assembly. This cable may chafe against the left rear brake line. Several temporary solutions to the problem are possible: Wrap the brake line in rubber tubing; replace it with an Aeroquip line; or use a brake line connector at the point of contact. A more permanent solution is to replace the brake line with a new one and, at the same time, either bend the rear axle bracket or relocate it to make sure that the flexible steel cable has adequate clearance and does not chafe the brake line.

PARKING BRAKE CABLE

To replace a broken parking brake cable, pull out the remaining center lead from the cable sheath. Cut the one good end off at the rear wheel. Get some 3/32 in outside diameter bare aircraft cable from your local private airport or Ace hardware shore. Lube the cable as it is inserted from the center to the wheel. To affix the cable to the rear wheel, double the cable through the hole vacated by the old cable, then clamp the new cable to itself with small cable clamps. Check for proper operation, adjust the free play, then readjust for cable stretch after the first few operations.

SECTION XI - WHEELS AND TIRES

This information comes from <u>Ferrari Circolare Tecnica No. 108/3</u>, DATED January 27, 1975.

	Low Speed		High Speed	
Pressures in lb/sq in	Front	Rear	Front	Rear
250 GTE 2+2				
Pirelli 185 x 15 Cinturato	24.3	30.0	28.5	32.9
Dunlop 700/15	24.3	30.0	28.5	32.9
330 GT 2+2				
Pirelli 210 x 15 NS	31.3	34.1	37.1	40.0
Pirelli 205 HR 15 Cinturato HS	31.3	34.1	37.1	40.0
Michelin 205 x 15	27.1	32.9	30.0	35.7
275 GTB				
Pirelli 210 x 14 HS	27.1	30.0	34.0	37.1
Dunlop 205 x 14 HR-SP	27.1	32.9	37.1	42.6
275 GTS				
Pirelli 210 x 14 HS	27.1	30.0	30.0	32.9
Dunlop 205 x 14 HR-SP	29.0	32.9	38.0	42.6
275 GTB/4				
Pirelli 210 x 14 HS	27.1	30.0	34.0	37.1
Michelin 205 VR 14 x or XWX	27.1	32.9	30.0	37.1
Dunlop 205 x 14 HR-SP	27.1	32.9	37.1	42.6
330 GTC/S				
Pirelli 210 x 14 HS	27.1	30.0	30.0	32.9
Michelin 205 VR 14 X or XWX	27.1	32.9	30.0	37.1
Dunlop 205 x 14 HR-SP	28.5	32.9	38.0	42.6
Firestone 205 VR 14 Cavallino Tubeless	27.1	31.3	31.3	37.1
365 GT 2+2				
Michelin 215/70 VR 15 X or XWX	27.1	32.9	34.0	40.0
Firestone 205 x 15 Cavallino Tubeless	27.1	32.9	30.0	36.0
365 GTC/S				
Michelin 205 VR 14 X or XWX	27.1	32.9	30.0	37.1
365 GTB/4				
Michelin 215/70 VR 15 X or XWX	34.0	38.0	40.0	44.1
365 GTC/4				
Michelin 215/70 VR 15 X or XWX	34.0	38.0	44.1	44.1
365 GT4/2+2				
Michelin 215/70 VR 15 X or XWX	40.0	47.0	45.5	49.8
DINO 206 GT				
Michelin 185 VR 14 X or XWX	27.1	31.3	27.1	31.3
Michelin 205/70 VR 14 X or XWX	27.1	31.3	27.1	31.3
DINO 246 GT				
Michelin 205/70 VR 14 X or XWX	27.1	31.3	27.1	31.3

WHEEL BALANCING

Have your wheels checked for proper balance at frequent intervals, especially if a front end vibration is noticed or chuck holes are frequently encountered. Most Bear alignment services can spin the wheels for dynamic balance. Alimite "on car" balancing can also be used – most large time centers have this type of equipment. Bubble or static balancing is not recommended.

When it comes to balance weights, there are certain precautions you should take. If you use rim weights – the type that are clipped on the edge – be sure you use balance weights that have the spring protected by a zinc coating. The use of weights that are not protected by a zinc coat can cause corrosion, especially on the cast or allow wheels. The problem is an electro-chemical reaction between the material of the wheel and the material of the retaining spring. The zinc coating prevents this.

Rim weights also have the tendency to fly off, and so to avoid both the problem of corrosion and the problem of lost weights, have the shop balancing your wheels use the adhesive stick-on type of weights. These are affixed to the flat side of the wheel.

TIRE MOUNTING

When mounting new tires, especially on new wheels, try and find a shop that will treat your wheels with care – preferably one that will mount the tires by hand as careless use of tire machines can damage our wheels. The cost may be high - $10.00 per wheel for mounting and dynamic balancing – but have you priced a new wheel lately?

WHEEL MOUNTING

Periodically remove the wheels from your Ferrari and grease the hub splines and tapers. If the wheels corrode on, they may become difficult to remove without a puller.

WHEEL CLEANING

When it comes to cleaning Ferrari wheels, especially wire wheels, each "expert" has his own favorite system and cleaning compound. Chrome Wheelspray, Aluminum Jelly, Spoke & Wheel Cleaner, and Gunk are just a few of the brand name products that come highly recommended. But no matter what you use, a good investment is a spoke and grille brush for reaching those hard-to-get-at places without busting your knuckles. As the name implies, a spoke and grille brush is good for chores other than just wheel cleaning.

For polishing the rims, try ordinary Wesley's silicon liquid auto polish. The anti-oxide agents in the polish lift the oxidations out quite well, and it leaves a tough wax finish to prolong the shine. If your rims need more help, try an electric drill-powered buffing wheel and some buffing compound to bring back the new look.

TIRE DRESSING

For refinishing the black on tires, there are several schools of thought. If you prefer using tire black, keep in mind the fact that some brands, such as Sears', leave a flat black color while others, such as Dupont's, leave a glossy black finish on the tires. The third choice is the one we prefer. ArmorAll not only cleans the tire but helps preserve and protect the rubber. It leaves no finish at all – only the clean black rubber shows.

KNOCK-OFF HAMMERS

McMaster Carr Supply Company, 2828 N. Pauline Avenue, Chicago, IL, Phone 312-281-1010, carries a complete line of lead knock-off hammers. They have sizes from ½ lb to 6 lb in stock. A good size for most wire wheels is a 4 lb, their part no. 5961A44. They also carry brass, fiber and aluminum hammers. FAF Motorcars stocks an all-purpose hammer with aluminum and plastic faces that protect very well against damage.

SECTION XII - ELECTRICAL SYSTEM

This section deals with those components of the Electrical System which are not exclusively applicable to the Ignition System. For those components which are specialized ignition components, see Part C of the Engine Section, page 51 of this manual

BATTERY

Battery failure and associated electrical failures contribute to a good percentage of Ferrari down time. Here are a few tips concerning the battery that may help avoid this.

To prevent battery terminal corrosion, install felt oil rings, available at most automotive parts houses, under each terminal. These inexpensive devices seem to work better than any other protective means, and they are not as messy as some products on the market.

Good electrical connections are of the utmost importance. Ground leads between the engine and the battery negative (-) terminals usually degenerate or are inadequate in most installations. A heavy gauge battery ground braid is recommended between the starter motor mounting bolt and the negative battery terminal connections. This will reduce the current path through the frame to the starter motor during cranking, and it will also help reduce the amount of ignition noise interference on the radio.

Check the specific gravity of the fluid in your battery from time to time, thus avoiding surprises when you really want to use the car. Small inexpensive battery hydrometers are readily available for less than $2.00. The following readings are for batteries at temperatures between 60°F and 80°F:

Specific Gravity	Charge State	Freezing Pt.
1.280 sp. gr.	100% Charged	-90°F
1.250 sp. gr.	75% Charged	-61°F
1.220 sp. gr.	50% Charged	-35°F
1.190 sp. gr.	25% Charged	-15°F
1.160 sp. gr.	Very low capacity	+1.6°F
1.130 sp. gr.	Discharged	+11°F
1.000 sp. gr.	Pure water	+32°F

A low charged or discharged battery will freeze if proper care is not provided. A frozen battery may split the case walls and cause acid damage if it is neglected. When storing a Ferrari for the winter, fully charge the battery and disconnect the cables. Better yet, remove the battery completely and store it, fully charged, in a cool, dry location.

Vibration can also cause battery failure, therefore a thin ¼ in rubber pad placed under the battery will greatly reduce the chances of damage.

VOLTAGE REGULATOR

ADJUSTMENT

All Ferrari 12 volt electrical systems should be set at 14.20 volts ±.20 volts at 75°F with a minimum electrical load and a 2,500 rpm engine speed.

Before attempting to adjust the voltage regulator, be sure the following conditions are present:

1. Battery is fully charged.

2. All accessories are turned off.

3. Fan belt (or alternator drive belt) is properly tensioned.

4. Surfaces on all relay contacts are clean.

5. Air temperature is neither very hot nor very cold.

To adjust the voltage regulator on an alternator-equipped car:

1. Operate the engine at 2,500 rpm for at least three minutes.

2. Use a small no. 2 Phillips screwdriver to adjust the control inside the regulator.

PRECAUTIONS

1. Never remove the regulator from its mounting surface while the engine is running. This will damage the regulator.

2. Never disconnect any of the regulator leads while the engine is running. This will damage the regulator.

3. Never remove the cables from the battery while the engine is running. This may damage the charging system.

4. Never polarize in any way an alternator system.

GROUNDING

The most common cause of voltage regulator failure on Ferraris is the lack of proper grounding for the regulator. The black ground lead from the voltage regulator is connected to a mounting point under the voltage regulator mounting bolt. Because this connection does not provide a reliable grounding point – rusting of the sheet metal fire wall, etc. – an additional ground path is recommended. Connect a lead wire of 16 to 18 gauge insulated wire from the black ground wire's junction with the regulator mounting screw directly to the engine block. This will insure that the black regulator ground lead is connected to a good ground source.

SUBSTITUTION

A domestic solid state voltage regulator can be substituted in place of the Marelli transistor regulator used on late model Ferraris equipped with alternators. One substitute is a Motorola 5-32 or TVR 12C31 (same unit) as used on Clark Equipment Company campers. This unit has a voltage adjustment capacity. Another substitute is a Motorola 8RB2006, which does not have the voltage adjustment feature. Both come factory adjusted to 14.20± .20 volts, per Ferrari specifications. Either of these units can be safely installed in a few minutes by following these instructions:

1. For safety in doing any electrical work, first disconnect the battery.

2. Be certain the black ground lead for the voltage regulator is connected to a good ground (see above). Failure to insure a good ground will only lead to failure of the replacement regulator.

3. Remove the old Marelli regulator.

4. Remove the plastic shell from the Motorola unit's cable.

5. Mount the Motorola regulator with the original nuts and bolts. The 5-32/TVR12C31 unit may be mounted using any two holes or, if exact mounting position is desired, drill a ¼ in (6 mm) hole centered between the two holes on the right side. On the 8RB2006 unit, mount with one bolt using any hole.

6. Connect the black regulator lead (ground wire) to the black cable from the Ferrari wiring harness.

7. Connect the green regulator lead (field wire) to the white cable from the Ferrari wiring harness.

8. Connect the third regulator lead (positive wire) – red on the 5-32TVR12C31, gray on the 8RB2006 – to the green cable from the Ferrari wiring harness.

9. Double check all connections and tape for insulation.

10. Check to make certain that the ground wires are in place and held down tight.

11. Reconnect the battery.

12. check the installation for proper regulation.

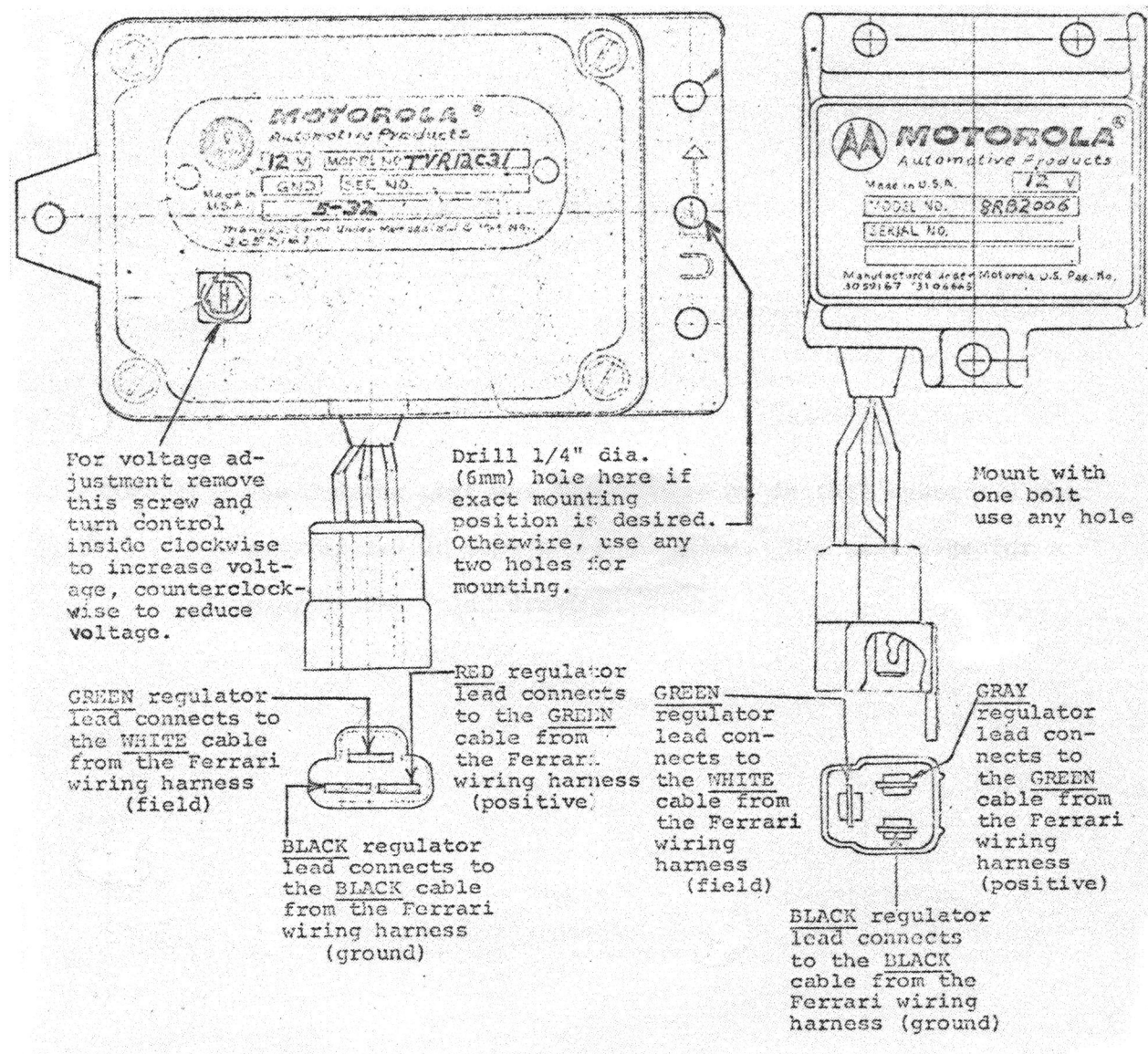

MARELLI ALTERNATOR SERVICING

The steps for checking, servicing, and rebuilding a Marelli alternator are as follows:

1. Remove the alternator from the vehicle.

2. Slowly turn the alternator pulley by hand to check the bearings.

3. Apply 12 volts DC between the field connection and the housing. The field should draw between 2.3 and 2.95 amperes. Rotate the front pulley to get a steady reading.

4. With 12 volts applied to the field, a small drag will be felt when the alternator's pulley is rotated by hand. This confirms the operation of the field circuit.

5. Remove the through bolts from the rear and slowly pull the rear housing and stator away from the front housing and rotor. Tap lightly with a wooden mallet if it is stuck.

6. Check each diode with a battery and light bulb to determine if a shorted or open diode is present. Between the diode mounting plate and the diode lead, the lamp should light in one direction then, when the leads are reversed, the lamp should not light. At this point it is not important which way they function.

7. Replace any diode that fails this test. Motorola Automotive Products dealers can supply diode kits to repair these. Replace diodes with read markings with Motorola part no. 2-1; replace those with black markings with Motorola part no. 2-2. These are 25 ampere 100V diodes that must be pressed in and out. Be certain you have the proper equipment – a small press – to handle the job. Use caution when pressing the diode in. Do not apply pressure to the lead or glass seal area. Solder the leads carefully and quickly to the diode lead. Trim lead to length if necessary. Check the diodes to be sure the test light functions properly.

8. Check for broken or shorted (bare) leads on the stator assembly. Strip, crimp, and resolder broken leads; tape bare leads if possible.

9. If the stator is blackened or charred, try to obtain a replacement.

10. Apply 12 volts DC between the copper slip rings at the rear of the rotor. A field current between 2.3 and 2.45 amperes should be read. If not, a new rotor is in order.

11. Polish the slip rings to a smooth copper finish with #400 emery paper.

12. If the bearings are noisy or damaged, replace them with new ones. Two SKF6202 are the usual bearings. Use a small arbor press to remove and install the front – most automotive machine shops can supply and install this bearing. New bearings are pre-greased. If the old bearings need grease, pluck out the seals, clean the balls in lacquer thinner, and grease with Chevron BRB #2. Carefully replace the seals.

13. For brushes, refit with new sets, usually available from Ferrari dealers, or substitute GM alternator brushes with a little trimming. Compress the brushes into the holders with your fingers. Insert a straightened paper clip through the small hole in the rear housing to retain them during assembly.

14. Refit the font and rear housings together, and remove the paper clip retainers. Torque the through bolts to 35 in lb.

15. A replacement for the large power transistor in the Marelli voltage regulator is the Motorola SP441 or 2N1167A.

REPLACING GENERATORS WITH ALTERNATORS

When it comes time to replace the generator on late model Ferraris with pulley-driven generators, an alternator substitution can be made for less than the price of a new generator.

Motorola makes several kits that easily adapt to Ferrari use. Their kit A35N12, rated at 35 amperes, is the least expensive yet is adequate for general replacement. Kit A40N12, rated at 40 amperes, costs a little more but is recommended for hard-starting, low-mileage Ferraris that require rapid battery replenishment. Kit A55N12, rated at 55 amperes, is even more expensive but is best for vehicles that are air conditioned or telephone equipped.

These kits come with everything needed – a solid state voltage regulator, brackets, cables, nuts and bolts, etc., as well as complete instructions.

The solid-state Motorola voltage regulator supplied with these kits, R2-2, should not be wired directly to the Ferrari wiring harness as was possible when replacing Marelli voltage regulators with Motorola 5-32/TVR12C31 or 8RB2006 voltage regulators. Instead, use the cable harness supplied with the kit as it is designed to electrically match the Motorola installation. When using the Motorola supplied cable harness with the complete Motorola kit, it is okay to mount the regulator under the hood. But the R2-2 should not be mounted in place of the old Marelli regulator on the firewall.

The yellow lead on the R2-2 should be connected, using the read lead supplied, to the positive (+) battery side of one of the ignition coils. This small current is used to start or excite the alternator and will not interfere with the vehicle operation. The other Motorola voltage regulators do not have and do not require this lead.

REPLACING MARELLI ALTERNATORS WITH MOTOROLA ALTERNATORS

Replacement of the alternator only in vehicles which were originally equipped with a Marelli alternator is quite simple. Instead of purchasing the entire kit, all you need is the alternator, an adaptor kit (Motorola no. 18-3) and a pulley (Motorola no. 7-1). Also, if your Ferrari happens to be one with a rearward facing alternator, order the Motorola no. 7-9 reversed (ccw or counterclockwise) rotation fan to insure proper cooling.

The same conditions apply to the applications and current ratings as for the kits. Motorola no. 10-118 (8AL200F) is an alternator rated at 35 amperes, no. 10-113 (8AL2016K) is rated 55 amperes. On very late model Ferraris with heavy electrical loads it may even be necessary to use a higher rated system. Motorola has them as well.

Motorola alternators work well with properly functioning Marelli voltage regulators. The only wiring change that needs to be made is with the terminations that connect to the rear of the alternator. Marelli uses push-on blade connections for outputs, while Motorola uses studs. Therefore, cut off the two large blade terminals from the heavy leads and replace them with a ¼ in ring terminal lugs. The smallest (field) lead uses a blade terminal, just push it on to the field terminal of the alternator. The regulator terminal of the alternator is not used. The black lead connects to the negative or ground terminal, and the white or red (large) cable connects to the positive output terminal.

Some small washers may be needed to align the belt adjustment bar. Check for good alignment with the crankshaft pulley, and retighten the belt after a few miles.

AVILABILITY OF MOTOROLA ALTERNATORS

Motorola alternators are available at most American Motors dealers, but the kits and accessories are only available from Motorola dealers. You also may be able to find a dealer or distributor who stocks rebuilt alternators. They are less expensive and work just as well.

AMMETER/VOLTMETER

Some early Ferraris did not have a method of keeping tabs on the charging system, such as an ammeter. Because an ammeter requires a wiring change, and does not tell the entire electrical story, a voltmeter can be used.

Stewart-Warner markets a small, 2-1/8 in outside diameter, expended scale (10-16 VDC) voltmeter. By connecting a <u>fused</u> wire from the battery to the meter, constant monitoring of the battery condition can be obtained. Since the meter draws only a few milliamperes, it will not cause a noticeable discharge over long periods of time.

WIRING

When following the Ferrari wiring diagrams, these color conversions may be helpful:

COLOR	COLORE
Black	Nero
Green	Verde
Brown	Marrone, Bruno
White	Bianco
Tan	Concia, Nocciola
Clear	Puro
Blue	Azzurro, Blu
Red	Rosso
Orange	Arancio
Yellow	Giallo
Violet	Viola
Purple	Porporina
Gray	Gregio
Silver	Argento
Light	Chiaro
Dark	Scuro

When wiring a vehicle, use a good, heavy gauge, stranded automotive cable, such as Belden appliance wire, or Belden Hypalon primary wire. Low temperature household or hobby wire with PVC insulation may melt or cut through, causing additional problems. The following current limitations should be observed (these are minimums):

        10A use 18 Gauge wire
        15A use 16 Gauge wire
        22A use 14 Gauge wire
        29A use 12 Gauge wire
        40A use 10 Gauge wire

When running a wire through a bulkhead, use a rubber grommet to prevent cut through. All leads conducting battery current should be fused.

FUSES

If you ever have occasion to replace an electrical fuse, you may find it difficult to locate the ceramic slug type with indented silver wire thread supplied on Ferraris.

An ideal replacement fuse is not made by Buss in several sizes: 7, 8 15 and 16 amps. They are designated GBC-7, etc., and are of the glass tube variety but with pointed end caps and are of the correct length to replace the original ceramic slug type. One source for these Buss fuses is your SAAB dealer.

Fuses are also available from your local VW dealer in 8 and 16 amp sizes. Complete kits of 10 are available from J.C. Whitney/Warshawsky & Co. One kit contains seven 8 amp and three 16 amp fuses and costs less than $1.00. Another kit contains two each 8 amp, 25 amp (17 x 7 mm), 25 am (25 x 6 mm), and 16 amp, and one each 35 amp and 50 amp. It costs less than $1.75. Check the Volkswagen pages of their catalog.

Another source of fuses to fit Ferraris is Littlefuse of Des Plaines, Illinois.

LUCAS ELECTRICAL COMPONENTS

When Lucas electrical parts go bad, try Joseph Lucas of North America for replacements – the same folks you saw for Girling brake parts.

FAF Motorcars is a stocking warehouse for Lucas items that were used on Ferraris, and carry everything that is available from Lucas.

LUCAS SPARE PARTS

FERRARI   Italy

Dino 206 G.T. Coupé (body by Scaglietti)
- Switch ... 108SA ... 35657

330 G.T.B. (body by Scaglietti)
Windshield wipers
- Motor ... 16W ... 75681A
- Rack ... — ... 54701531
- Wheelbox (2 off) ... — ... 72822A
- Arm (2 off) ... — ... 54702927
- Blade (2 off) ... — ... 54702255

330 G.T. 4 litre L.H.D. (body by Pininfarina No. 242)
Windshield wipers
- Motor ... 6WA ... 75561A
- Rack (cut to 40½") ... — ... 743235
- Wheelbox (2 off) ... — ... 72772A
- Outer casing
  - Motor to wheelbox ... — ... 54700217
  - Wheelbox to wheelbox ... — ... 54717234
  - Short, wheelbox ... — ... 740746
- Grommet ... — ... 740811
- Arm (10° R.H. crank) ... — ... 54717530
- Blade (anti-wind lift) ... — ... 54714391
- Switches (5 per car) ... 108SA ... 35657B
- Lighting ... 45SA ... 35656B
- Fan motor (2 off) ... 3GM ... 78378
- Grommet (4 per motor) ... — ... 748843
- Nut (4 per motor) ... — ... 54131266
- Washer (4 per motor) ... — ... 131670
- Nylock nut (1 per motor) ... — ... 54130206

330 G.T. 4 litre R.D.H. (body by Pininfarina No. 244)
As above with the exception of:
- Arm (10° L.H. crank) ... — ... 54717531

275 & 330 G.T.S. 3 & 4 litre L.H.D. 'Spyder' (body by Pininfarina No. 243)
Windshield wipers
- Motor (early) ... 6W ... 75561A
- Motor (later) ... 14W ... 75641B
  (use 75664 and 54702585)
- Rack (cut to 32 5/32") (early) ... — ... 743216
- Rack (cut to 32 5/32") (later) ... — ... 743221
- Wheelbox (2 off) ... — ... 72771
- Outer casing (early)
  - Motor to wheelbox ... — ... 54718610
  - Wheelbox to wheelbox ... — ... 54718611
  - Short, wheelbox ... — ... 740746
- Outer casing (later)
  - Motor to wheelbox ... — ... 54703367
  - Wheelbox to wheelbox ... — ... 54718611A
  - Short, wheelbox ... — ... 54702605
- Arm ... — ... 54712026
- Blade ... — ... 54719460
- Cable adaptor ... — ... 54939680
- Switch (5 per car) ... 108SA ... 35657B
- Switch, lighting ... 45SA ... 35656B
- Fan motor (2 off) ... 3GM ... 78378
- Grommet (4 per motor) ... — ... 748843
- Nut (4 per motor) ... — ... 54131266
- Washer (4 per motor) ... — ... 131670
- Nylock nut (1 per motor) ... — ... 54130206

FERRARI—continued   Italy

275 & 330 G.T.S. 3 & 4 litre L.H.D. 'Spyder' (body by Pininfarina No. 243)—continued
Optional equipment
- Alternator ... 11AC ... 54021168
- Control box ... 4TR ... 37423

275 & 330 G.T.S. 3 & 4 litre R.H.D. 'Spyder' (body by Pininfarina No. 247)
As L.H.D. 'Spyder' with the exception of:
- Arm ... — ... 54712042

275 & 330 G.T.C. 3 & 4 litre L.H.D. Coupé (body by Pininfarina No. 246)
Windshield wipers
- Motor (early) ... 6W ... 75561A
- Motor (later) ... 14W ... 75641B
  (use 75664 and 54702585)
- Rack (cut to 32 5/32") (early) ... — ... 743216
- Rack (cut to 32 5/32") (later) ... — ... 743221
- Wheelbox (2 off) ... — ... 72771
- Outer casing (early)
  - Motor to wheelbox ... — ... 54718610
  - Wheelbox to wheelbox ... — ... 54718611
  - Short, wheelbox ... — ... 740746
- Outer casing (later)
  - Motor to wheelbox ... — ... 54703367
  - Wheelbox to wheelbox ... — ... 54718611A
  - Short, wheelbox ... — ... 54702605
- Arm, driver's side ... — ... 54717906
- Arm, passenger's side ... — ... 54716247
- Blade ... — ... 54719460
- Cable adaptor ... — ... 54939680
- Switch ... 108SA ... 35657B
- Switch ... 45SA ... 35656B
- Fan motor (2 off) ... 3GM ... 78378
- Grommet (4 per motor) ... — ... 748843
- Nut (4 per motor) ... — ... 54131266
- Washer (4 per motor) ... — ... 131670
- Nylock nut (1 per motor) ... — ... 54130206
Optional equipment
- Alternator ... 11AC ... 54021168
- Control box ... 4TR ... 37423

275 & 330 G.T.C. 3 & 4 litre R.H.D. Coupé (body by Pininfarina No. 248)
As above with the exception of:
- Arm, driver's side ... — ... 54717907

365 G.T. Altair 4 litre 2+2 L.H.D. (body by Pininfarina No. 251)
- Switch ... 108SA ... 35657B
- Switch, hazard warning ... 45SA ... 35916A
- Relay ... 6RA ... 33222E
- Relay ... 6RA ... 33231E
- Dimming relay ... 11RA ... 33301A
- Brake failure } ... 18RA ... 33305A
- Checklite unit }
- Adaptor and cable assembly ... — ... 54951935
Windshield wipers
- Motor ... 14W ... 75638B
  (use 75664 and 54702598)
- Rack (cut to 40½") ... — ... 743235
- Wheelbox (2 off) ... — ... 72771
- Arm ... — ... 54701173
- Blade, passenger's side ... — ... 54701324
- Blade, driver's side (Europe) ... — ... 54702496
- Blade, driver's side (U.S.A.) ... — ... 54702255

365 G.T. Altair 4 litre 2+2 R.H.D. (body by Pininfarina No. 252)
As above with the exception of:
Windshield wipers
- Motor ... 14W ... 75641B
  (use 75664 and 54702585)
- Rack (cut to 40½") ... — ... 743227
  (use 743235)
- Blade, passenger's side ... — ... 54701324
- Blade, driver's side ... — ... 54702496

IGNITION SWITCH

If you ignition switch runs warm due to the heavy electrical load from accessories, try the Motorola 9-5 high power switch (relay) to help carry the current. It comes with instructions.

HEADLAMPS

Some early Ferraris with single headlamps have a tendency to lose the rims on the street when one hits a bump. It is a good idea to lace a small piece of nylon fishing line through the small drain hole in the rim and secure it to the bucket. This is especially applicable to the Lusso, which has a tendency to lose these rims.

If you lose the rims from your Lusso, see your local Peugeot dealer. They have rims and headlights that match in stock and moderately priced.

Peugeot dealers are also the source of two assemblies – part nos. 620129 or 620143 – that will adapt sealed-beam headlights to the Ferrari 250 GTE 2+2. These same assemblies take quartz-halogen or Marchal "Equilux" reflectors as well if you are interested in more authentic appearance. Their Marchal part no. 58060 matches the original Ferrari units.

For replacement driving lamps on the four-headlight 330 GT 2+2, an aircraft landing light made by GE will work well. A small notch must be cut in the mounting ring to clear the index nub on the sealed beam. As with all high power driving lights (quartz, etc.), use a relay to take the load off of the switch. A GM horn relay will do a good job – this same relay can also be used to replace Ferrari relays for horn, overdrive, and lights.

TAILLIGHTS

Some rear lights in the Ferrari 250-330 series have two or three single filament bulbs, thus leaving the appearance of burned out lamps when viewed at night. These single function lamps can be replaced with dual filament bulbs, resulting in increased lighting and good appearances.

Purchase the proper dual filament stoplight replacement sockets from your local parts house. Next, remove the center contact section from them and insert this new section into the old shell from which you have removed the old contact assembly. Determine which lead operates the lower power filament of the 1034 or 1157 bulbs. Connect all of these leads to the wire that powered the parking or taillights.

The 1034 or 157 bulbs will not insert into the Ferrari lamp shell without a small modification. Since the standard bulb has both key pins at the bottom of the base, one of the 1034 or 1157 lamp pins – the one farthest from the base – will need to be filed off. One pin is sufficient for proper operation.

Connect the brightest lamp lead to the stop light wire and the turn signal to another. Locate each function in its proper area, that is, turn signals above or outside stop lights.

BACK-UP LAMPS

A good replica for the Ferrari back-up lamp assembly – the single one at rear center, below the bumper – is a unit from the Capri. This lamp, complete with bulb and cable, costs less than $10.00, is part no. DORY15500-A, and can be ordered from any Lincoln-Mercury dealer who carries parts for the Capri.

TURN INDICATOR/PARKING LIGHTS

Lenses and trim rings for front turn signal lights as used on the 250 GT Berlinetta Lusso are available from Lucas or Austin-Healey parts dealers.

Altissimo parking/turn indicator lamp assemblies used by Ferrari on 250 GTEs, Lussos, GTBs, etc. were also used on the popular Alfa Romeo Guilietta Veloce. For replacements, see your local Alfa dealer.

MISCELLANEOUS BULBS

Alfa Romeo dealers are also a possible source of supply for light bulbs used in dash instruments, as are Mercedes-Benz dealers. This type of hardware is pretty much standardized on the metric system, and the European manufacturers have all agreed on certain bulbs for certain applications.
An exact replacement instrument panel bulb is a no. 363, available at large electronic supply houses. For an emergency substitute, use the lower power no. 53 bulb, available at many local service stations. These will also fit the side turn signal indicator.

SECTION XIII - BODYWORK AND TRIM

PAINTING

For any Ferrari owner contemplating the repainting of his pride and joy, we recommend the reading of Technical Tip 1C-1, printed in the Ferrari Club of America's periodical, The Prancing Horse, No. 31. If you are going to be happy with a $49.95 local "Ajax Bump and Brush plus lifetime around-the-block guarantee" paint job – and we can't really believe you will be – then you needn't bother to read Paul Elbert's description of how to get a better than new finish. But if you are interested in having a truly professional finish applied to your car, whether you are going to do it yourself or have it done for you, then by all means read and heed Paul's tips and suggestions.

COLOR

No current Ferrari production car is painted "Ferrari Racing Red", according to Dick Fritz of Luigi Chinetti Motors. A good color match for Ferrari painted Ferrari race cars is found in an ordinary domestic spray can of SPARVAR bright red, No. S-130, Federal Standard 595 No. 11136, manufactured by Valley Forge Products Company, Norristown, PA. No, we are not suggesting that you repaint your Ferrari with a batch of aerosol cans, but the purchase of one should allow you to make a color chip that can be matched by a competent custom painter.

Older racing Ferraris were painted in a deeper red color than that in use more recently. The hue, called "Rosso Corsa" or racing red, was prevalent in the early 1950s, and it is not exactly clear just when it was replaced. The Ditzler firm (see below) has had the formulation for this red and gave it no. DBE 70797. The formulation was for lacquer.

"Rosso Chiaro Ferrari" or Ferrari light red, manufactured by Glidden Salchi, S.P.A. (see below) appears to be what is often thought to be Italian racing red. It is a very clear, bright red, and the color many owners would like to match when repainting sports Ferraris. The color experts at GM Styling advise that no American manufacturer of paints puts out such a clear red, as it is thought to be unstable by our firms. From the paints available at GM, the closest color to match this Rosso Chiaro Ferrari was 1966 Corvette Red. It lacks the brilliance of the Ferrari red, however.

Gerry Sutterfield's prize-winning and immaculate 166 MM was painted with Bahia Red from Porsche – fitting since Gerry is a Porsche-Audi dealer. It comes very close to matching the Rosso Chiaro Ferrari. It is Dupont No. 8365AH.

DITZLER PAINT

Pittsburgh Plate Glass Co., PPG Industries, P.O. Box 5090, 7 Oak Station, Detroit, MI 48235, manufactures original Ferrari colors and lists these formulas in their Ditzler Imported Car Colors catalog – the page dealing with Ferrari is reproduced below. They have offices and distributors in most large cities in the United States. For quick information, call the automotive refinishing department of PPG at 313-444-4760 in Detroit, Michigan.

MADE IN ITALY

YEAR	PAINT CODE	COLOR NAME	GENERAL DESCRIPTION	CHIP NO.	DITZLER CODE
1963-71	2041.A BIA	Off White (Tetratema Bianco)	Gray White – much lighter and cleaner than	6	8625
1971 & Prior		Dark Ronald Black			9000
1963-71	2033.6A AZZ	Blue Poly (Hyperion Azzurro)	Medium Gray Blue – much cleaner, lighter than (with Poly)	14	13093
1963-71	48	Ribot Blue Poly	Medium Blue – lighter, bluer than (with Poly)	3	13094
1963-67	45	Silver Blue Poly	Medium Silver Blue – Gray – lighter, bluer than	16	13095
1965-71		Bright Blue Poly (Gladiateur Azzurro)	Bright Blue – much brighter and bluer than	96	13773
1968-71		Gainsborough Celeste Poly	Silver Blue – slightly lighter than	16	13770
1968-71		Tourbillon Blue Poly	Dark Blue – darker, bluer than	47	13771
1968-71		Caracalla Blue Poly	Dark Blue – deeper blue	25	13772
1963-67	2451.S NOC	Tan (Nocciola)	Medium Tan – darker – no Poly	113	22614
1968-71		Colorado Brown Poly	Bronze Gold – darker, richer, browner than	19	23149
1963-71		Kelso Gold Poly	Dark Gold – darker than	89	23150
1963-71	2025.S MAR	Cordovan (Marrone)	Dark Brown – browner than	84	22612
1965-71		Nashrullah Gold Poly	Medium Beige – darker (with Poly)	24	23151
1963-67	2152.S GRI	Dark Gray (Grigio Scuro)	Dark Gray – darker than	69	32496

ORIGINAL FINISH – ENAMEL & ACRYLIC LACQUER

YEAR	PAINT CODE	COLOR NAME	GENERAL DESCRIPTION	CHIP NO.	DITZLER CODE
		Medium Gray (Grigio Medio)	Medium Gray – lighter than	62	32497
1963-67	19249	LeSancy Silver Gray Poly	Medium Gray Silver – lighter than	67	32771
1968-71	36	Mahmoud Gray Poly	Medium Gray – darker (with Poly)	70	32779
1968-71	330	Oriello Gray Poly	Medium Dark Gray – darker (with Poly)	37	32780
1968-71		Molvedo Turquoise	Medium Dark Green – slightly lighter	114	43957
1968-71		Blenheim Green Poly	Medium Dark Green – darker, richer than	52	43998
1968-71		Bahram Green Poly	Medium Light Green – darker, richer than	64	43999
1963-69		Seabird Green	Dark Green	65	44000
1966		Bull Lea Maroon	Maroon	75	50710
1968-71		Blandford Violet	Purple Violet		50814
1968		Race Car Red	Light Red – slightly darker than	33	70797
1963-68		Red	Bright Red – richer, darker	99	71568
1966		Red	Dark Red – much darker	33	71727
1968-71	19374	Rosso Red	Medium Dark Red – (redder than 71727)		71745
1968-71		The Tetrarch Cream	Pale Cream – lighter than	13	81729
1968-71		Man O'War Yellow	Pale Yellow – cleaner than	105	81730

GLIDDEN SALCHI S.P.A. PAINT

No less than 27 colors are available in acrylic enamels for contemporary Ferraris from Carrozzeria Seaglietti, produced by Glidden Salchi SPA of Milano.

Name	Number	Description
Rosso Cordobo Metallizzato	106-R-7	Dark Red Metallic
Rosso Robino	106-5-12	Medium Red Metallic
Nocciola Netallizzato	106-M-27	Bronze Metallic
Oro Chiaro Metallizzato	106-Y-19	Clear Gold Metallic
Bleu Notte Metallizzato	106-A-31	Light Blue-Green Metallic
Celeste Chiaro Metallizzato	106-A-26	Clear Blue Metallic
Celeste Metallizzato	106-A-16	Blue-Gray Metallic
Assurro Metallizzato	106-A-32	Silver-Blue Metallic
Verde Pino Metallizzato	106-C-30	Pine Green Metallic
Verde Medio Metallizzato	106-G-29	Medium to Light Green Metallic
Grigio Ferro Metallizzato	106-E-8	Iron Gray Metallic
Grigio Notte Metallizzato	106-E-28	Warm Silver Gray
Argenio Auteil	106-E-1	Silver
Marrone Ferrari	20-M-189	Dark Red-Brown
Amaranto Ferrari	20-R-118	Medium Maroon Red
Rosso Ferrari	20-R-187	Medium Red
Rosso Chiaro Ferrari	20-R-190	Bright Red
Nero	20-B-50	Black
Bleu Ultrascuro	20-A-174	Navy Blue
Bleu Ferrari	20-A-185	Dark Blue
Assuro La Plata	20-a-167	Clear Light Blue
Verde Searo Ferrari	20-G-186	Very Dark Green
Grigio Brighton	20-E-166	Dark Gray
Bianco	96-W-157	Off White or Light Gray
Bianco Polo Park	20-W-152	Pure White
Avorio	20-Y-153	Ivory
Giallo Fly	20-Y-191	Bright Yellow

REMOVING PAINT

For removing those stray sprays of paint from glass, rubber, gaskets, and chrome trim, OC steel wool does a good job without scratching the surface. This extra-fine steel wool can be used to polish chrome trim and plastic parts.

MISCELLANEOUS PAIANTING TIPS

To refinish the black wrinkle finish on the cam covers or other parts, use VHT, Cal Custom, or other good brand of wrinkle spray paint. Strip the old paint off with paint remover and dry the surfaces. Heat the parts in an oven or with a heat lamp to about 250°F. Spray the black wrinkle paint on the hot surface, and heat again at about 250°F for twenty minutes or more.

VHT silver spray paint makes a nice refinish or touch-up for aluminum engine parts. VHT black spray paint works very well on exhaust headers and pipes. After applying VHT paints, be sure to warm the engine up. This has the effect of baking the paint on the parts.

PROTECTING YOUR PAINT JOB

Mequiars Competition Car Wax is now being sold to the public. This great hard-to-get wax provides one of the nicest finishes possible. The one pound tub is no. ME-22 and is available from Vilem B. Haan, Inc., 10305 Santa Monica Blvd., West Los Angeles, CA 90025.
Porzelack polishes, wax, and chrome cleaner – recommended for the finish of a Rolls-Royce – also do an excellent job of preparing your Ferrari for a concourse. The complete line of Porzelack products is available from FAF Motorcars.

To protect your spotless finish from the elements and/or curious people who like to put their fingerprints on shiny cars, try a car cover. There are numerous different types on the market, at widely varying prices, made of different materials, with different properties. MG Mitten, Vilem B. Haan, and, of course, FAF Motorcars all have car covers for the Ferrari. FAF Motorcars' covers come in 16 (at last count) different patterns and four different fabrics.

Two other protective devices for your Ferrari are:

Fender covers – available with Ferrari emblem for those who really like to show off, but the use of any protective fender cover is strongly recommended whenever you are working under the hood.
"Bras" protect the nose of the Ferrari when on the road, and are available for most late model Ferraris.

BODY HARDWARE

PININFARINA CREST

The Pininfarina crest has adorned the flanks of more than just Ferraris. For replacements, try one of these other body styles like the Alfa Romeo.

WINDSHIELD WIPERS

Wiper blades for many late model Ferraris are available from Lucas – or a Lucas dealer. The last time we checked blades were still available for the 275 and 330 GTS, 330 GTC, 365 GT 2+2, 365 GTB/4 and GTC/4.

Replacement blades for other types – especially the 275 GTB and GTB/4 – may be difficult to find, or require some compromise. The original blades have plastic linkages placed almost horizontally rather than vertically, thereby reducing frontal area and consequently reducing lift at high speeds. Most substitute blades do not have this feature.

The compromises you can make are:

You can install a substitute make of blade that looks good but which may still lift off at high speed, and then drive slowly in the rain.

You can install the make of blade that employ an airfoil to combat the wind lift, but they don't look very good.

You can find a Ferrari dealer who stocks replacement blades – but the cost is often quite high.

Finally, you can do what one preserving and patient Ferrari owner did, and order directly from the factory. He ended up with a set, at a modest cost, that were similar to the original but use metal rather than plastic linkages. They were manufactured by "Arman & C."

KEYS AND LOCKS

Bullis Lock and Key Service, 4340 W. Addison Street, Chicago, IL 60641, 312-545-8033, can make keys to fit Ferrari locks. They can also modify tumblers to match all locks to one key.

To help prevent car theft, install a double pole single throw (DPST) toggle switch in some hidden place, and wire it to short out each distributor (points) to ground. Every little bit helps.

EXTERIOR REAR DECK HINGES

The external type rear deck hinges, as used on the 275 GTB and GTB/4, are the same as the hood hinges used on the Alfa Romeo Guiletta Spyder.

WINDSHIELDS

New windshields for Ferraris can be obtained from.
Specialized Auto Glass
P.O. Box 370
Newhall, CA 91322
805-259-2882 or 213-874-4685

They have in stock the molds for 250 GT Berlinetta Lusso, 275 GTB and GTB/4, 365 GTB/4 Daytona, 500 Superfast, and Dino 206/246.

If you need a windshield for a Ferrari other than those listed, they can make one up in curved safety glass as long as you have the outside edge for a pattern.

Stick-on hidden windshield antennas, like General Motors', are available from Sears. They are easily applied to the inside surface of the front or rear glass, and really work, although not as well as a standard antenna mast.

WINDSHIELD WASHER

A replacement for the 330 GT 2+2 windshield washer is the unit made by Robert Bosch, part no. WW712, 12 volt. It works well, is small, and well weather-proofed.

RUSTPROOFING

No matter where or when you drive your Ferrari, you can have a rust problem. Avoiding salted roads or the seashore will not avoid the rust problem – rain and condensation also cause rust, they just take longer to do you in.

You can rustproof your car yourself. Texaco puts out, in aerosol cans, a rustproofing compound called "Compound L". Texaco service stations will apply this for you – if you want it all over the disc brakes, engine, transmission, etc. But you can do it yourself, and insure that the job is done right.
The first step is to acquire some of the compound from a Texaco distributor. You have to buy it on a company name, as they can not sell to the retail trade. Of course, you might be able to talk your local Texaco retail dealer out of some, but at a higher price.

Next, be sure the car is dry. Three days in a heated garage or sunshine with low humidity is sufficient. Use whatever means you have to get the car off the ground. Remove the wheels and cover the brakes with rags or aluminum foil – no paper, it acts like a blotter.

Use a stiff brush to scrape all of the dirt and sand you can reach, and compressed air to clean the hard to reach places.

Once you have the underside clean, start spraying. Spray the compound on every surface, seam, and joint you can find, especially around welds, headlight wells, etc. If your car is undercoated, spray right on the undercoating – the compound will soften the undercoating, making it more effective, and will work its way through the creep into the metal surface. If there is no undercoating, spray on the bare metal. This works almost as well, but requires more frequent applications.

The amazing thing about this compound is that it not only prevents rust, but will stop a rusting piece from further rusting. The Porsche Club of America had quite an article on it from their factory, with the factory recommending it instead of redoing the undercoating. It is harmless to rubber, wiring, chrome, and so forth. If you get some on the paint, clean it off with a solvent.

A common problem on many Ferraris is excess moisture inside the door panels. Some Ferraris do not have the rain protection that American cars have, therefore a small modification can be made.

Remove the inside door panels and check to see if plastic splash sheets are installed. If not, obtain some heavy gauge plastic material. Using rubber cement or contact cement, fasten the plastic material inside the door just behind the door panel. Make sure it does not show when the panel is reinstalled.

If the inside of the door is not undercoated, spray a heavy coat of undercoating material on all surfaces before installing the plastic – or treat with Texaco's Compound L. Be sure not to gum up the window cable or door latch mechanisms.

WINDOW CHANNELS

If the window channel material in your doors is becoming worn or leaky, try replacing it with a stock universal replacement. J.C. Whitney/Sarshawsky & Co. stock this. Remove the glass and/or old channel with care and cement the new replacement in with 3M weatherstrip cement. Lube the track with silicon spray for easy operation.

GRILLE RUBBER

The molded rubber channel (gasket) that fits around most Ferrari grilles is available from:
Fullerton Air Parts
4010 w. Commonwealth Avenue
Fullerton, CA 92633

This small rubber piece can also be used around the Lusso bumperettes, and on some pieces of interior trim.

RUBBER MOLDINGS

All types of door seals, trim edgings, trunk seals, and even some odd window moldings, are available from FAF Motorcars. This includes some rubber moldings/seals that have been remanufactured since the original equipment is no longer available.

275 GTB HEADLAMP LENSES

275 GTB Headlamp lenses are available for $47.00 a pair from Fullerton Air Parts, address above.

275 GTB/4 TAILLIGHT LENSES

Taillight lenses for the later 275 GTB/4 (after about Serial No. 10401) are the same as the taillight lenses used on the Fiat 850.

INTERIOR TRIM

HANDLES, ETC.

250 GTE 2+2 window cranks can be made using cranks from the Fiat Pininfarina Cabriolet (1500). Remove 3/32 in from the splined shank of the Fiat crank, then use their mounting hardware and chrome trim.

Inside door handles for the 275 GTB/4 are the same as those used on the Fiat 850, although chromed. These may need to be remachined and grooved on the splined area to fit the Ferrari cross pin.

TRIM SCREWS AND WASHERS

Trim Screws are stocked by most automotive parts houses. Doorman products makes a complete line of metric fasteners, available singly or in kits at many automotive parts houses.
A quick source for small chrome plated screws is the local hardware store or Sears. These wood screws are not very strong, but they will help complete the décor at very low cost.
For cup washers to be used on interior trim, try the local radio parts store. These chrome or nickel plated washers are available for #6, #8 and #10 screws.

BRASS AND COPPER

For cleaning brass fittings and hardware, a product called Mint-Luster will do a good job. This chemical will clean all copper and brass parts immersed in it, all by itself. Mint-Luster is sold by large sporting good stores for cleaning the brass on rifle cartridges, and some coin shops carry it for coin rejuvenation.
After cleaning the part, spray it with clear lacquer prior to refitting, This will preserve the shiny clean appearance.

SEAT BELTS

Nice matching seat belt sets can be made from late model <u>rear</u> seat belts from General Motors. Remove the GM crest from the buckle and epoxy a small tie tack Ferrari emblem on its place. The seat belts are available in many colors, but be sure you get rear seat belts, to avoid the shoulder harness straps found on the front seat belts.

SOUNDPROOFING

For soundproofing the floor and headliner areas, try the headliner insulation from a 1972 Chevrolet Camaro. This material was designed to cut noise by the use of a new thin material. The neoprene foam on the back of Ozite carpets makes a chap floor and door soundproofing base.
When selecting a material for insulating, be sure that it will not hold water, i.e., closed cell, etc. Materials that hold water, such as foam rubber, wood and fiberglass, will only contribute to the rust problems of the vehicle.

RADIOS

Radios for late model Ferraris (such as 365 GTB/4 Daytonas) or any other model with a small radio opening are available from Porsche/Volkswagen/Audi dealers. These are manufactured by Motorola, and can only be purchased from a dealer. All three radios are similar, but differ slightly in trim. The Porsche and VW units have their names stamped on the front panel – this can be easily removed. The Audi unit has only their multiple circle emblem. While all three units are AM/FM/MX stereo, the VW radio is the least expensive. Part numbers are:
    VW – 1VW2114
    Audi – 1AU2125
    Porsche – 1PE 2127

LEATHER CARE

Dry and weathered leather can be softened with a product called Lexol. This preparation is low cost and does a good job of restoring oils to leather. However, it has a tendency to discolor some lighter shades of leather, so test it first on an inconspicuous place.

Connolly Hide Food, made especially for leather by the famous English leather upholsterers, Connolly Bros. (Curriers) Ltd., is an excellent treatment for your Ferrari leather. It cleans, nourishes, and protects the leather.

If your leather interior is too far gone for Lexol, Hide Food, etc., we recommend the kits to restore badly dried, cracked and discolored leather that are available from:

>The Clausen Company
>1055 King George Road
>Fords, NJ 08863

These kits are available in three sizes, depending upon the amount of leather you need to restore, and the individual components are also available. The most expensive kit, "for larger cars," costs only $33.50 and for this you get a crack filler, solvent cleaner, rejuvenator oil, low-gloss paint-like material, and the necessary sandpaper and brush.

The standard kits come in tan, dark brown, maroon, dark blue, dark green, cherry red, and black. They can also match their kits to your color sample for $3.00 per color per kit. If you want a custom match, cut a piece of leather off the bottom of your seat and send it to them.

This is the best solution we have come across to leather that was too far gone for Hide Food, short of a completely new upholstery job.

HEATERS

The heater blower motor made by Smiths and used on Ferraris made in the mid-1960s (330 GT 2+2 and 330 GTC for instance) was also used on MGs of the same vintage.

A common complaint on some Ferrari models is the lack of heat in the winter months. There are two ways to increase the hot water circulation in your heater, thereby increasing the heat available.

The least expensive method is to replace the ½ in inside diameter hose with 5/8 in inside diameter heater hose. Use a good grade of gasket cement or silicone rubber adhesive at each connection point, and two hose clamps.

More expensive, but more effective, is to splice a small electric pump into the heater system. Jabsco Products Division of ITT corporation manufactures a small electric pump called the Mini-Puppy. This pump, when inserted into the heater input water line, will greatly increase the heat output. The pump has standard garden hose make connections, therefore ½ in inside diameter garden hose female connections will be needed for the hookup. The pump can be mounted in any convenient location near the proper heater hose – it does not require shock mounting – and is very quiet in operation.

For a 6-volt operation, use Jabsco no. 8850; and for a 12-volt system, no. 8860. The 12-volt pump may require a small .1 ohm 20 watt resistor to prevent the impeller from overheating during continuous operation. This resistor is available from most electronic parts stores, part no. Ohmite Brown Devil 1802A, style 200-20, .1 ohm 20 watt. Connect the black lead from the pump to a good ground, and the read lead to the resistor. The outer side of the resistor (which gets warm) connects to an on-off switch, then wire the other terminal of the switch to the ignition switch, etc.

The manufacturer of the Mimi-Puppy is:
> Jabsco Products Division
> 1485 Dale Way
> Costa Mesa, CA

Contact them for the dealer or distributor in your area if you have any trouble locating a source for the pump.

SECTION XIV - MISCELLANEOUS

Here, as a finale, we have various tuning tips and maintenance techniques which either did not exactly fit in any of the previous sections, or which should have been in an earlier section but inadvertently got left out.

METRIC FASTENERS

For metric fasteners, hardware, etc., try any dealer – such as Volkswagen, Fiat, Honda, etc. – whose products are made to metric standards. Other sources for metric goodies include:

McMaster Carr Supply Company
2828 N. Paulina Avenue
Chicago, IL

Metrics, Inc.
6140 Waygate Boulevard
Golden Valley, MN 55416

Metrics & Multistandard Components Corp.
198 Sawmill River Road
Rimsford, NY 10523
     Or
822 West 47th Street
Chicago-Lyons, IL 60534

And, as mentioned earlier, doorman Products, which are available at most automotive parts houses, carry a complete line of metric fasteners.

For some non-critical fasteners, you can re-tap some USS and SAE nuts and bolts. For 5 mm nuts and bolts, usually used on trim and interior applications, rethread a #10-32 nut or bolt. For 8 mm (coarse) nuts and bolts, use a 5.16 NC. Of course, to do this you will first have to get a metric tap and die sit. J.C. Witney/Warshawsky & Co. sell inexpensive sets, as does Sears.

Many SAE sockets and wrenches will function as metric tools in an emergency. Try to use a six point socket to minimize the chances of rounding the head off.

    2mm = approx. 3/32
    3mm = approx. 1/8
    4mm = approx. 5/32
    6mm = approx. ¼
    8mm = approx. 5/16
    11 mm = approx. 7/16
    13mm = approx. ½
    14mm = approx. 9/16
    15mm = approx. 5/8
    17mm = approx. 11/16
    22mm = approx. 7/8
    24mm = approx. 15/16
    37mm = approx. 1-7/16

CHASSIS LUBE FITTINGS

In order to grease vehicles with the European hex head grease fittings, a special hard-to-locate adaptor is required. A well-made hex grease fitting adaptor, their part no 413, is available from:

    Wilco
    P.O. Box 1128
    Rochester, NY 14603

This fitting has a metric pipe thread, and will not mate directly to a standard American grease gun. With a small modification, a complete head and hose assembly can be fabricated.

Obtain a flexible grease gun hose, usually available at Sears. Place the adaptor in a vise, and screw the hose into the threads three full turns. Considerable effort must be applied, as the screw pitch is not the same. The result will be a strong, tight connection that should not leak. This assembly will now thread directly on to a standard grease gun.

If you would rather change your grease fittings to American Zerk fittings, check with your BMW or Fiat dealer for Zerk fittings that have the property (8 x 1.0) metric thread. FAF Motorcars also has these fittings.

It is a good idea to cover your grease fittings with a guard – this keeps them dirt and moisture free, and makes them easy to find. One source for these is a product called Protek, made by

    Bold Industries
    P.O. Box 1308
    Melrose Park, IL 60160

For hex head grease fittings, specify Protek #7; for Zerk fittings, specify Zerk Type.
FAF Motorcars also has plastic grease guards available.

LUBRICANT DRAIN PLUGS

To prolong the life of the engine, transmission, differential, etc. it is advisable to add a small magnet to these drain plugs. Small rod magnets can be epoxied on to a clean, oil-free drain plug. Allow plenty of time to dry before replacing the plug.

If some difficulty is encountered in removing filler or drain plugs, a small hammer impact wrench can be used. Standard ½ in drive SAE sockets can be used with these drivers to loosen tight bolts, etc., without stripping the threads. Always use a six point socket if possible as these have less of a tendency to round off the head than a twelve point socket. When replacing the plugs, be certain the threads are clean, the gasket (preferably a new one) is in place, and apply a small amount of grease to the threads. Always use safety wire if possible. A new length is required each time.

When installing anew plug, always check to be sure it fits property. For instance, ion some 250 series engines, new replacement oil drain plugs have an interference with the cooling fins on the oil pan. Screw the plug in carefully, and note if the plug flange hits the oil pan. If so, remove the plug and grind or file this flange down, being careful not to damage the threads.

METRIC STANDARDS

One advantage you have as a Ferraristi is the fact that you are already familiar with the metric system of measurement – the rest of the country is slowly being forced to learn this system as the United States makes the conversion.

Some of the more common conversion factors, to help you read your European gauges, Ferrari literature, or what have you, are as follows:

    LENGTH
    1 centimeter (cm) = 0.3937 inch
    1 kilometer (km) = 0.621 mile
    1 millimeter (mm) = 0.3937 inch
    1 meter (m) = 39.37 inches
    1 meter (m) = 3 feet, 3.37 inches
    1 inch (in) = 2.54 centimeters (exact)
    1 mile (mi) – 1.609 kilometers
    1 inch (in) = 25.4 millimeters (exact)
    1 foot (ft) = 0.3048 meters (exact)

    VOLUME
    1 cubic centimeter = 0.061 ci
    1 liter = .264 U.S. gallons (gal)
    1 liter = 1.057 U.S. quarts (qt)
    1 liter = 2.113 U.S. pints (pt)
    1 cubic inch (ci) = 16.387 cc
    1 U.S. gallon = 3.785 liters
    1 U.S. quart = 0.946 liters
    1 U.S. pint = 0.473 liters

WEIGHT
1 gram (g) = 0.035 ounce, avdp
1 kilogram (kg) = 2.205 pounds
1 ounce avoirdupois (oz avdp) = 28.350 g
1 pound (lb) = .4536 kilogram

TEMPERATURE
To convert degrees Centigrade (°C) to degrees Fahrenheit (°F), multiply by nine, divide by five, and add 32 degrees.

To convert degrees Fahrenheit to degrees Centigrade, subtract 32 degrees, multiply by five, and divide by nine.

MISCELLANEOUS

In addition to the common measurements, the following conversions are particularly helpful to Ferrari owners:

    For tire pressure
    1 atmosphere (stm) – 14.70 pounds per square inch (psi)
1 psi = .068 atm

    For speed
    1 kilometer per hour (kph) = .621 miles per hour (mph)
1 mph = 1.609 kph

    For torque
    1 meter-kilogram (mkg) = 7.233 foot-pounds (ft lb)
1 ft lb = .1383 mkg

    For oil pressure
    1 kilogram/square centimeter = 14.22 pounds per square inch
    1 pound per square inch = .070 kilogram/square centimeter

    On older cars
    1 meter pressure = 1.42 pounds per square inch

O RINGS

The Parker Seal Company lists about 500 different "o" rings in their catalog, in both English and metric sizes. This variety should fit most of the standard requirements of "O" rings. They are available in most areas from jobbers. If unavailable in your area, write for their catalog and distributor listing. Their address:
    Park Seal Company
    10567 Jefferson Boulevard
    Culver City, CA 90230

TOW ROPE

To prevent being stranded, a good security blanket is a nylon tow rope. Sears sells a convenient nylon tow strap. This item stows easily in the trunk and is much more gentle than a chain.

BEARINGS

When it comes to trying to locate replacement ball and roller bearings for your Ferrari, all we can say is good luck. Many of the bearings used on Ferraris are not interchangeable with readily available standardized sizes.

With luck, you might be able to find a replacement or substitute, usually an SKF bearing, at a bearing supplier in a large city. To try and obtain a replacement bearing, either bring the old, defective one with you to the dealer, or get the number stamped on the side seal of the bearing.

When removing and installing bearings, use care and the property tools, such as pullers. Never put pressure on the outer race if the bearing is held in by the inner race, nor pressure on the inner race if the bearing is held by the outer race.

Most sealed bearings are pre-lubricated by the manufacturer. Exceptions are the open bearings running in oil such as used in the transmission and rear axle. If the sealed bearings are to be repacked, use a good quality bearing grease. For loose fitting bearings that have worn the retaining surfaces, try Loc-Tite's Bearing Lok. This compound will retain bearings with a small amount of retainer wear.

BEARING SEALS

Seals for the front and rear axle bearings are the same as used by M.G. Bring your old parts in for a comparison.

CABLES

Chevrolet has a flexible cable used on late model cars for the throttle linkage. This flexible tube and cable assembly is Chevrolet part no. 9840654. It can be cut to the required length, then soldered or clamped in place.

If you have trouble with a sticking or stiff choke or vent actuating cable, try lubricating them with speedometer cable lube or a commercial motorcycle chain lube. These lubricants contain graphite and a vehicle that evaporates, leaving the parts free of sticky oil. NEVER USE OIL. It attracts dirt, and may cause future problems.

FERRARI PEOPLE

For additional information and/or help with your Ferrari related problems, you might try contacting one of the following. This is by no means an all-inclusive list, and is not intended as an endorsement or recommendation of those listed, nor is the exclusion of anyone to be taken as a non-recommendation.

CLUBS

Ferrari Club of America
Dyke W. Ridgley, Membership Chairman
1474 Greendell Drive
Decatur, IL 62526
Publishes quarterly The Prancing Horse with technical tips, and monthly News Bulletin. Annual meeting plus more-frequent regional meetings.

Ferrari Owners' Club (U.S.A.)

Edwin K. Niles, Membership Secretary
346- Wilshire Blvd., Suite 1007
Los Angeles, CA 90010
Publishes bi-monthly magazine Ferrari with occasional technical tips, and monthly newsletter. Monthly meeting in California, others, less frequently, in other areas.

Ferrari Owners' Club (U.K.)
Geoff Ward, Secretary
Cedar Court, 9 The Fair Mile
Henley-on-Thames, Oxfordshire
England
Publishes quarterly magazine Ferrari, which is available to non-club members by subscription.

Club Ferrari Belgio
Serge-Marie Orban, Secretary
43 rue Goffart
1050 Bruxelles
Belgium
No publications as yet.

Australian Ferrari Register
Barney Govan-Smith, Secretary
P.O. Box 203
Shepparton 3630, Victoria
Australia
Quarterly newsletter for members only.

Club Ferrari France
Jess G. Pourret, General Secretary
9 rue Gustave Courbet
Paris 16e
France

Quarterly magazine Ferrari, in French.
Ferraristi Svezia
Rein Thomson, Secretary
Tvarskedet 26
S-415 06 Gothenburg
Sweden
Publishes Ferraristi Svezia 3-4 times a year, in Swedish.

Bugatti Ferrari Owners' Club Switzerland
Edy Strebel, Jr., Secretary
Buschweg 15
3097 Liebefeld
Switzerland
Publishes Ferrari News, available by subscription to non-members.

Southern Equitorial Ferrari Automobile Club
Stan Wesselink, Secretary
P.O. Box 6653
Johannesburg
South Africa
No regular publication.

DEALERS/SERVICE/PARTS

Algar Engerprises, Inc.
1100 W. Swedesford Road
P.O. Box 455
Paoli, PA 19301

Archway motor Imports, Ltd.
610 Manchester Road
Manchester, MO 63011

Auto Classic Ltd.
10591 Bechler River Avenue
Fountain Valley, CA 92708

Autohaus, Inc.
742 Cushing Highway
Cohasset, MA 02025

Auto International
1944 West North Lane
Phoenix, AZ 85021

Automobiles International
8117 East 46th Street
Tulsa, OK 74145

Bavarian Italian Motors Ltd.
4731 South State Street
Salt Lake City, UT 84107

Bobcor Performance Corporation
5363 Main Street
Willilamsville, NY 14221

Rob de la Rive Box
P.O. Box 5253
Effingen
Switzerland

California Imports
3920 Stevens Creek Boulevard
San Jose, CA 95129

The Checkered Flag
Vineland, NJ

Chinetti-Garthwaite Imports, Inc.
1100 W. Swedesford Road
P.O. Box 455
Paoli, PA 19301
(Eastern U.S.A. Distributors)

Luigi Chinetti Motors, Inc.
600 W. Putnam Avenue
Greenwich, CT 06830

Luigi Chinetti Motors, Inc.
New York Showroom
301 East 57th Street
New York, NY 10022

Classic Motors, Inc.
1046 N.W. 71st Street
Oklahoma City, OK 73116

Competition & Sports Cars Ltd.
355 W. Putnam Avenue
Greenwich, CT 06830

Courtesy Pontiac, Inc.
227 W. Broadway
West Memphis, AR 72301

Robert Cressman Foreign Cars
222 S.W. 25th Street
Fort Lauderdale, FL 33315

Diagnosis & Service
3134 Santa Monica Boulevard
Santa Monica, CA 90404

European Motor Garage, Inc.
1244 Wayne Avenue
Daytona, OH 45410

European Motors Ltd.
580 S. State Street
Salt Lake City, UT 84111

F.A.F. Motorcars, Inc.
3861 Stephens Court
Tucker, GA 30084

Ferrari Denver
2166 15th Street
Denver. CO 80202

The Ferrari Store
1351 E. Pomona Street
Santa Ana, CA 92705

Fong's, Inc.
16 Third Street, N.E.
Atlanta, GA 30308

Alf Francis, Inc.
410 S. emporia
Wichita, KS 67202

Grand Prix Louisville
6339 Upper River Road
Harrods Creek, KY 40027

Grand Prix Motors
150 Lakeside Avenue
Seattle, WA 98122

Grand Touring Cars
2302 East Magnolia Street
Phoenix, AZ 85034

Grand Touring Motors
3054 North Lake Terrace
Glenview, IL 60025

Graypaul Motors Ltd.
Charnwood Road, Shepshed
Loughborough, Leicestershire
England

Griswold Company
1485 San Pablo Avenue
Berkeley, CA 94702

Grossman Motor Car Corporation
336 Route 59
West Nyack, NY 10994

Hollywood Sports Cars
5766 Hollywood Boulevard
Hollywood, CA 90028

Italia Auto Sport, Inc.
7401 West 63rd **Street**
Overland Park, KS 66202

JTS Motorcars, Inc.
1072 Taft Street
Rockville, MD 20850

Knauz Continental Autos, Inc.
1044 North Western Avenue
Lake Forest, IL 60045

Wes Lasher Porsche-Audi-Ferrari
5830 Florin Road
Sacramento, CA 95823

Love-Thomas Motors
1341 Kapiolani Blvd.
Honolulu, HI 96814

Joe Marchetti
519 Milwaukee Avenue
Chicago, IL 60622

Marque Motors
139 Huntington Drive
Monrovia, CA 91016

Modena Racing Co., Inc.
770 11th Avenue
New York, NY

Maranella Concessionaires
Tower Service Station
Egham By-Pass, Surrey
England

Newport Sports Cars
3100 West Coast Highway
Newport Beach, CA 92660

Stanley Nowak
12 Kimball Place
Mt. Vernon, NY 10550

Ogner Porsche-Audi-Ferrari
21301 Ventura Boulevard
Woodland Hills, CA 91364

Orange Motors of Miami
500 N.W. 36th Street
Miami, FL 33127

Precision Motors
7814 North Central Expressway
Dallas, TX 75206

R.A.B. Motors
595 Francisco Boulevard
San Rafael, CA 94901

Ramsey Motor Company
1154 Del Monte Avenue
Monterey, CA 93940

Riverside Sports Cars
3600 Van Buren
Riverside, CA 92503

Schwing Motor Company, Inc.
3326 Keswick Road
Baltimore, MD 21211

SCU Industries, Inc.
3509s Schoolcraft Road
Livonia, MI 48150

Pete Sherman Exotic Cars
190 Shell Point W.
Maitland, FL 32751

Simpson Automobili
5818-A Star Lane
Houston, TX 77027

Specialty Motorcars
3200 N. Washington
Arlington VA

Taylor Rolls-Royce, Inc.
1314 S. Dixie Highway
West Palm Beach, FL 33401

Thorobred Motorcars, Inc.
1008 N. Randolph Street
Arlington, VA 22201

Ron Tonkin Gran Turismo
1737 S.W. Morrison
Portland, OR 97205

Waldron Motors
Boca Raton, FL

Wide World of Cars
233 West Route 59
Nanuet, NY

Woodnorth, Harry
1650 N. Bosworth
Chicago, IL

Modern Classic Motors
201 West 2nd Street
Reno, NV 89501
(Western U.S.A. Distributors)

Yonge Steeles Motors, Ltd.
7079 Yonge Street
Toronto
Canada

Motorcraft, Ltd.
16 West 201 Thorndale Rd.
Bensenville, IL 60106

APPENDIX A - WEBER CARBURETOR DIAGRAMS

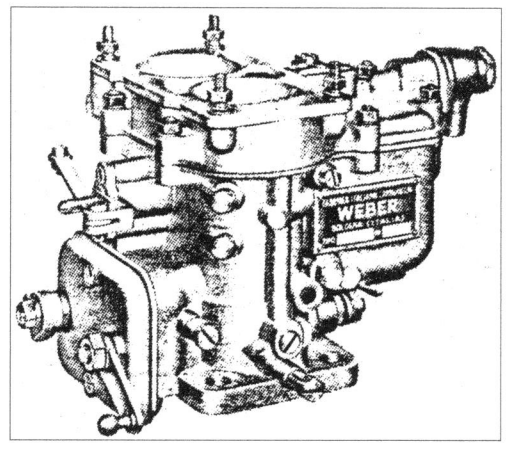

WEBER CARBURETORS
Types 36-40-42 DCF, DCL, DCZ
Type: twin choke downdraft
Intake pipe diameter in mm: 36 - 40 - 42
Starting device: with E.I. (E = Summer - I=Winter) control
Accelerating pump: metal piston
Extra power device: by valve
Metal: DCF: anticorodal aluminim (production ceased)
DCL: pressure cast anticorodal aluminum
DCZ: pressure cast zamae alloy

Some of the popular installations: Alfa Romeo 1900 - Bugatti 101 - Ferrari 166/212/250/340 - Fiat 8V -Lancia Aurelia B20/B22 - Pegaso Z 102

INTRODUCTION

The double choke downdraft carburetors of the DCF - DCL - DCZ type are obtainable with diameters at the height of the throttle valves of 36, 40 and 42 mm. thus permitting their use over a great range of engines. On these carburetors the device for governing the fuel mixture consists of two throttles mounted on two parallel shafts. These valves are kept in perfect relation by means of two geared segments mounted on the ends of the shafts and they open and close in counter rotation assuring a perfectly equal fuel distribution in either intake pipe. The carburetors of the DCF, DCL, DCZ type are provided with an accelerating pump and starting device; moreover, on request they can be supplied with the full power device fitted. The main intake pipes of this type of carburetor work independently one from the other, since each of them constitutes a complete single choke carburetor.

DESCRIPTION

The cross section in Figure 1 shows how the air arrives from the top, passes through the auxiliary Venturi (2) where it mixes with the the fuel coming out of the discharge tubes (3) and then, through the chokes (30) it is carried to the engine cylinders according to the opening of the throttle valves (28). From the fuel line connected with the carburetors by means of a suitable fitting, the fuel flows through the needle valve (11) into the float bowl (16) where the float (10), hinged to the pivot (13) controls the needle opening (12) and maintains the fuel level constant. From the float bowl the fuel controlled by the calibrated main jets (22) arrives at the emulsion tubes (4) by means of the pipes (23) from which mixed with the air arriving from the calibrated air adjusting screws (5) through the emulsioning tubes and discharge tubes (3) it reaches the carburation zone constituted by the
auxiliary Venturis (2) and the chokes (39). The purpose of the auxiliary Venturis is to increase the vacuum around the discharge tubes (3) and to carry the emulsified fuel to the center of the chokes (30) at their narrowest diameter so as to render the mixture more homgeneous with the advantage of a better distribution to the cylinders. For idling operation of the engine the fuel, by means of suitable pipes, is carried from the emulsioning tubes (4) to the calibrated idling jets (6) from which, emulsified with the air deriving from the calibrated holes (7) through the tubes (29) and the idling feeding holes (27) adjustable by means of conical screws, it arrives at the carburetor throttles chamber below the throttles where it mixes itself with the air which is sucked in by the engine vacuum through the small openings existing between the throttles chamber walls and the throttles when in idling position. From the tubes (29) the mixture arrives at the carburetor throttles chamber through the progression holes (26) situated in relation to the throttles and having the purpose of permitting smooth increases of the engine speed when starting from idle, when the throttles are opened.

The accelerating pump permits a regular increase of engine speed even when the throttles are suddenly opened.

In the carburetors of the DCF - DCL - DCZ type the accelerating pump is a metal piston (15) activated by the pump control shaft (8) through the lever with small roller (25) fixed to the shaft bearing the main throttles lever.

When closing the throttles, the lever (25) by means of the shaft (8) lifts up the piston (15); the fuel is then drawn from the float bowl into the pump cylinder through the intake valve (19). Opening the throttles, the shaft (8) remains free and the piston (15) is pushed towards the bottom of the spring (9); by means of the tube (17) the fuel is forced through the ball delivery valve (31) to the pump jets body (1) from which it is injected into the carburetor main intake pipes by means of suitable calibrated tubes. In order to vary the fuel quantity discharged by the accelerating pump, the carburetors of the DCl - DCZ type are provided with a pump exhaust screw (18) for the DCZ type the exhaust is obtained by means of a suitable hole made in the pump piston (15).

In the carburetors of the DCF - DCL - DCZ type the ball check of the delivery valve of the accelerating pump may be substituted by a needle valve (14).

In case of special need, that is when each carburetor intake pipe feeds three cylinders or more, the carburetors of the DCF - DCL - DCZ type may be supplied complete with the full power device constituted by the valve (24) and calibrated jets (20). With throttles completely open the piston (15) pushed towards the bottom by the spring (9) opens the full power valve (24) allowing the fuel calibrated by the jets (20) to pass from the float bowl to teh opening of the emulsioning tubes (4) through the intake valve (19) and the tubes (21) thus increasing the mixture strength drawin in by the engine through the auxiliary Venturis (2).

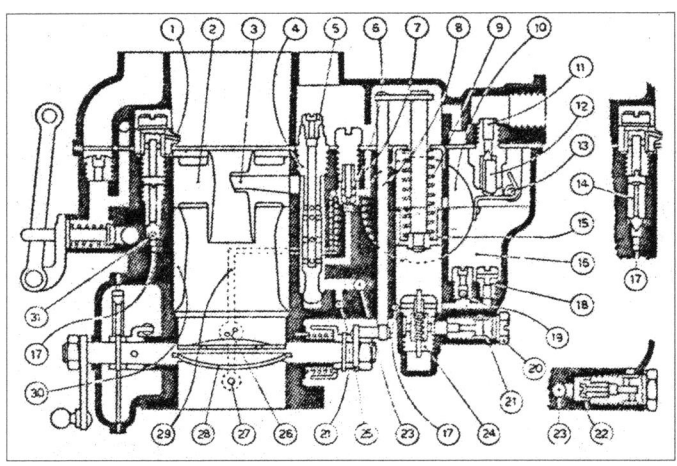

Figure 1

Descriptive Cross Section

1 - Pump jets body
2 - Auxiliary Venturi
3 - Discharge tube
4 - Emulsioning tube
5 - Air adjusting screw
6 - Idling jet
7 - Idling air hole
8 - Pump control shaft
9 - Pumping prologation spring
10 - Float
11 - Needle valve seat
12 - Needle for valve
13 - Float fulcrum pivot
14 - Needle delivery valve of pump
15 - Pump piston
16 - Float bowl

17 - Pump tube
18 - Pump exhaust tube
19 - Pump intake tube
20 - Full power jet
21 - Full power tube
22 - Main jet
23 - Jet-Emulsion tube pipe
24 - Full power valve
25 - Pump control lever
26 - Progression holes
27 - Idling hole to the intake pipe
28 - Throttle
29 - Idling mixture tube
30 - Choke
31 - Ball delivery valve

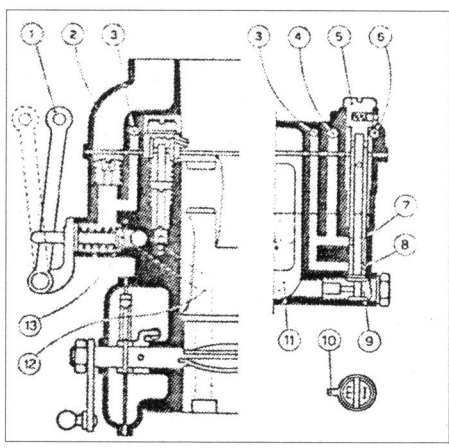

Figure 2

Descriptive Cross Section

1 - Starting valve control lever
2 - Starting air screw
3 - Starting mixture hole
4 - Starting air hole
5 - Starting control
6 - Air hole for starting control
7 - Hole for Summer mixture
8 - Hole for Winter mixture
9 - Starting jet
10 - Reference mark of the control on the carburetor cover
11 - Float bowl
12 - Starting mixture tube
13 - Starting valve

STARTING DEVICE - Fig. 2

The starting device allows a quick start when engine is cold. It is controlled from normal driving position by pulling a suitable knob on the instrument panel and should be released as soon as the engine reaches a sufficient temperature for regular running.

The fuel flowing from the constant level float bowl (11) through the calibrated jet (9) arrives at the housing tube (5) of the starting device. With the throttles in idling position the conical valve (13) is opened by the lever (1) the suction due to the engine under starter operation consents that the fuel, after a primary emulsification with the air coming through the holes (4) and (6) reaches the conical valve port (13) through the tube (3). This mixture is then further emulsified by air drawn through the calibrated screw (2) and is carried, by means of the tube (12), to the carburetor main pipes below the throttles.

For correct operation of the device it is necessary that the letter engraved upon the control (5), giving the weather conditions (E = Summer - I = Winter) should be in index with the reference finger (10) on the carburetor cover; the mixture formed by the fuel arriving from the jet (9) and the air arriving from the hole (6) is in this way fed by the calibrated hole (7) - Summer position - or by the calibrated hole (8) - Winter position - so that the device may supply the proper mixture for quick starting of the engine.

Sideview

1 - Fuel filter casing
2 - Starting mixture control
3 - Idling jet
4 - Auxiliary Venturi securing screw
5 - Choke securing screw
6 - Idling mixture adjusting screw
7 - Idling speed adjusting screw
8 - Idling mixture adjusting screw
9 - Inspection screw for progression holes
10 - Main jet
11 - Full power jets
12 - Starting jet
13 - Bolt securing fuel filter casing

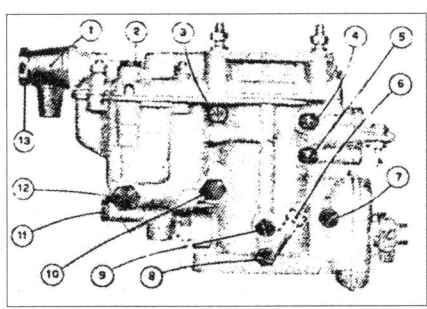

Figure 3

In order to allow the user to visualize the external pieces forming the carburetors of the DCF - DCL - DCZ type described in Figures 1 and 2, a sideview of the carburetor is shown in Figure 3 from which is seen that said pieces are readily accessible and demountable.

The carburetor being symmetrical in respect to a plane passing between the main pipes, said view denotes also the other side of the carburetor with the exception of the starting jet that, as already mentioned, is unique.

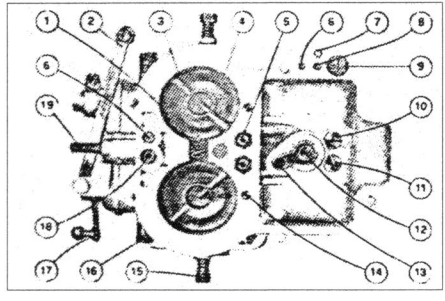

Figure 4

In order to indicate the position of the internal pieces of the carburetors of DCF - DCL - DCZ type Figure 4 shows the plan view of said carburetor without the cover.

Plan View

1 - Pump jets body
2 - Starting control lever
3 - Auxiliary Venturi
4 - Chokes
5 - Emulsioning tubes completely with air adjusting screws
6 - Starting mixture tube
7 - Starting emulsion air hole
8 - Starting emulsion tube
9 - Starting control

10 - Pump intake valve
11 - Pump exhaust screw (for DCL - DCZ only)
12 - Accelerating pump
13 - Pump control shaft
14 - Bushings for idling air
15 - Idling mixture adjusting screws
16 - Idling air adjusting screws
17 - Throttle control lever
18 - Starting emulsion air screw
19 - Starting valve

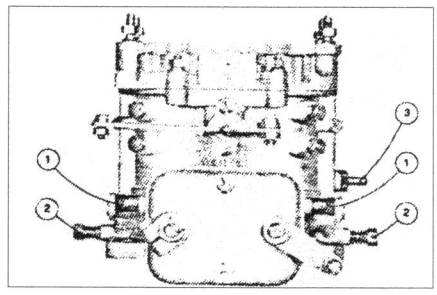

Figure 5

TUNING FOR IDLING

In the carburetor of DCF - DCL - DCZ type (Figure 5) the idle adjustment device consists of the idling speed adjusting screws (1) and the mixture adjusting screws (2). The screws (1) control the amount of throttles opening syncronized by means of the geared segments; the screws (2) with the conical end maintain the proper air-fuel ratio for smooth engine operation by controlling the quantity of the mixture from the idling jets and its mixture with the air drawn in by the engine. The screws (2) can be arranged as indicated in the sketch (6) of Figure 3.

Tuning for the proper idle must be carried out with the engine warmed setting first the minimum opeing of the throttle valves by means of the screws (1) adjusting it to a position to prevent the engine from stalling under all conditions. Then turn the screw (2) to obtain the best mixture strength for the fastest, stable and smoothest running at that throttle's valves position. Finally the throttle valves opening can tehn be reduced further to obtain the most suitable idling speed.

In Figure 5 is also shown the boss (3) for the eventual connection of the automatic spark advance. For fitting on engines having said device, the carburetors of DCF - DCL - DCZ type can be supplied, at request, completed with said connecting piece.

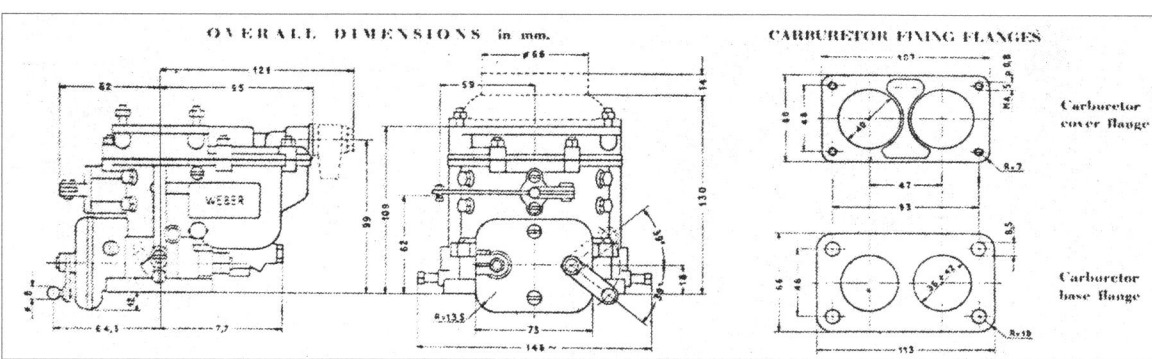

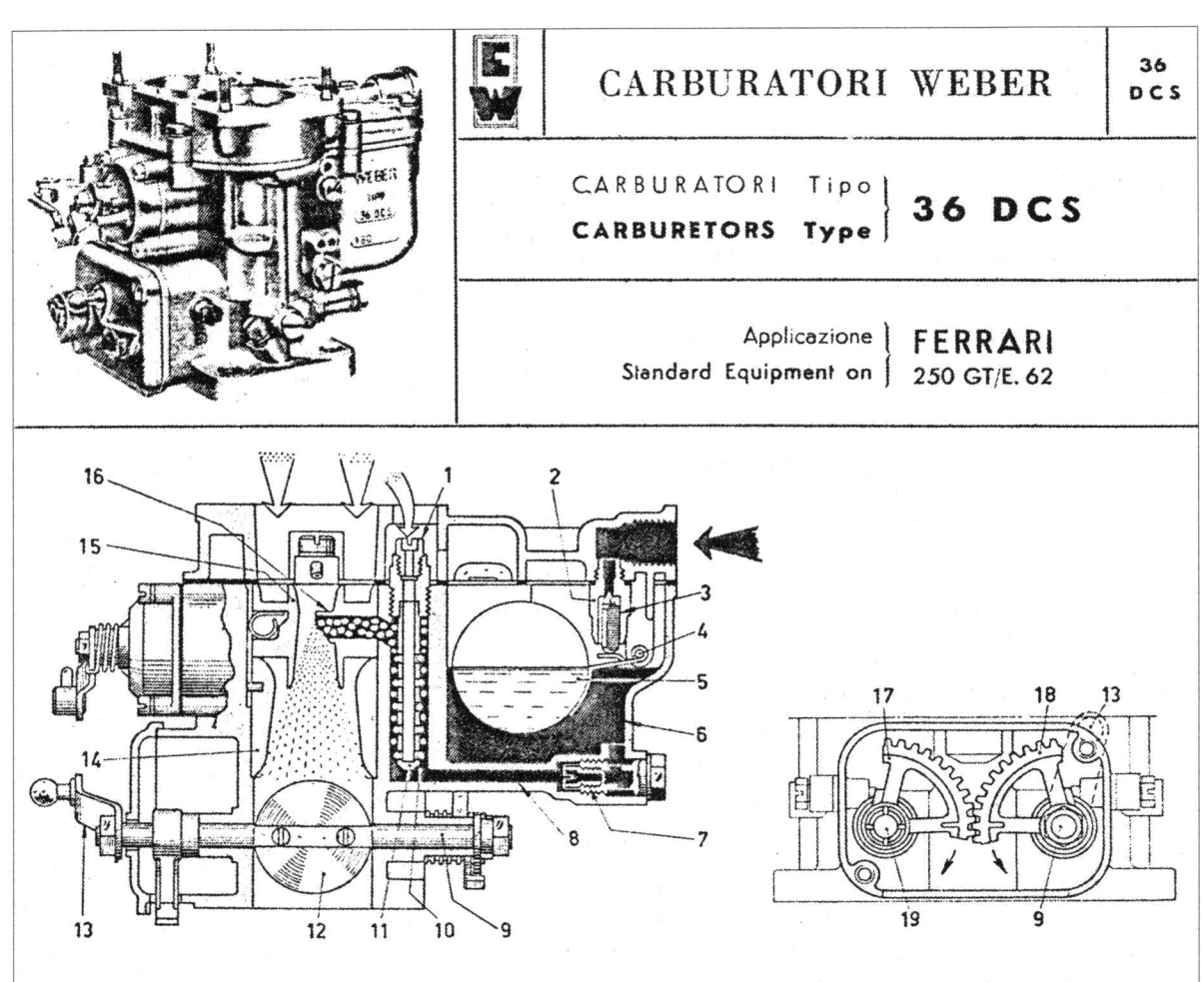

Figure 1

NORMAL RUNNING - Fig. 1
The fuel through the needle valve (2) passes to the bowl (6) where the float (5), articulated in the trunnion (4), regulates the needle opening (3) in order to keep the level of the liquid constant. From the bowl (6), through the main jets (7) and ducts (8), the fuel reaches the wells (10) where, mixed with the air from the orfices of the emulsioning tubes (11) and coming from the air connector jets (1), through the nozzles (16), it reaches the carburetion area, consisting of the venturi (15) and the secondary venturi (14).

Fig. 1 shows the device for synchronized opening of the throttles. Acting on lever (13), the throttles (12) are syinchronously controlled by means of toothed sectors (17) and (18) fixed to spindles (9) and (19), and open in opposite directions, so making sure of perfectly even feeding to the inlet ducts.

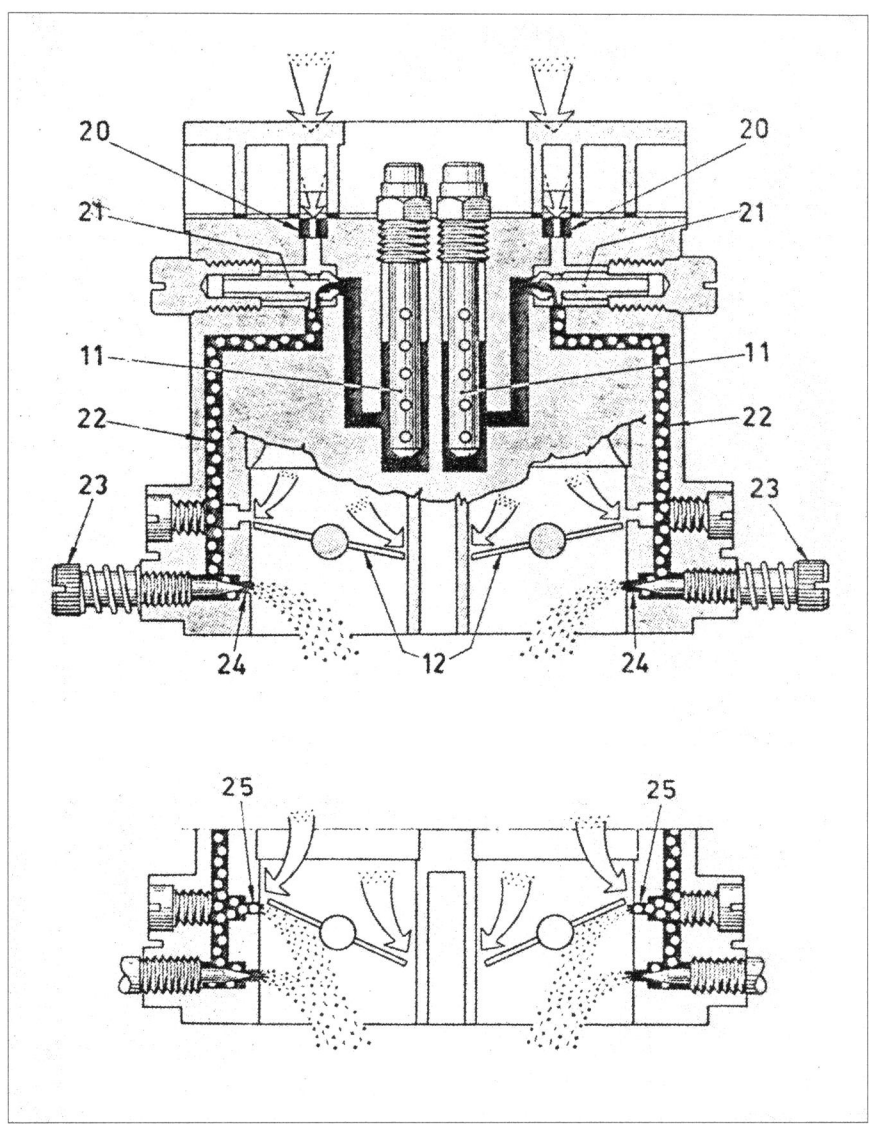

Figure 2

IDLE SPEED AND PROGRESSION - Fig. 2

From the primary emulsioning tube wells (11) the fuel passes to the idle jets (21) from which, emulsioned with the air coming from the calibrated bush (20), through ducts (22) and the idle feed orfices (24), the last being adjustable by means of screws (23), it reaches the carburetor ducts downstream of the throttles (12).

The mixture also reaches the ducts from progression holes (25) placed on a level with the throttles, so allowing a regular increase in angular speed of the engine starting from idling speed.

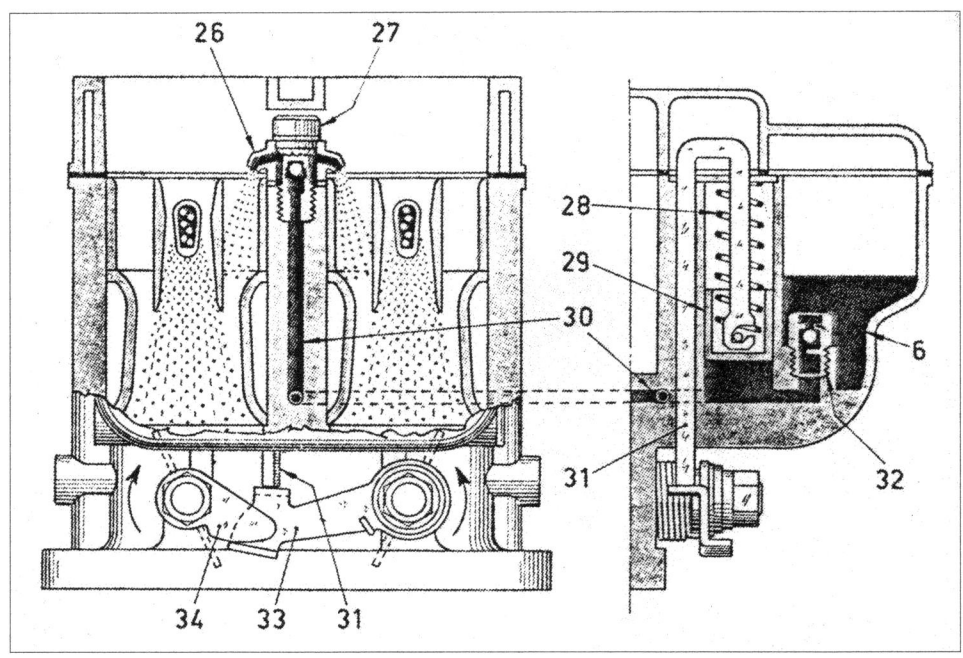

Figure 3

ACCELERATION - Fig. 3

Closing the throttles, lever (33) through the rod (31), raises the plunger (29). The fuel is drawn from the bowl (6) into the cylinder of the pump through the inlet valve (32). By opening the throttles, lever (34) lowers lever (33), so freeing rod (31). The plunger (29), through the action of spring (28), is pushed downwards, along the ducts (30) the fuel is injected through valve (27) and the calibrated pipes of the jet pump (26) into the carburetor ducts.

The inlet valve (32) may be supplied with a lateral calibrated orfice which discharges any excess fuel into the well.

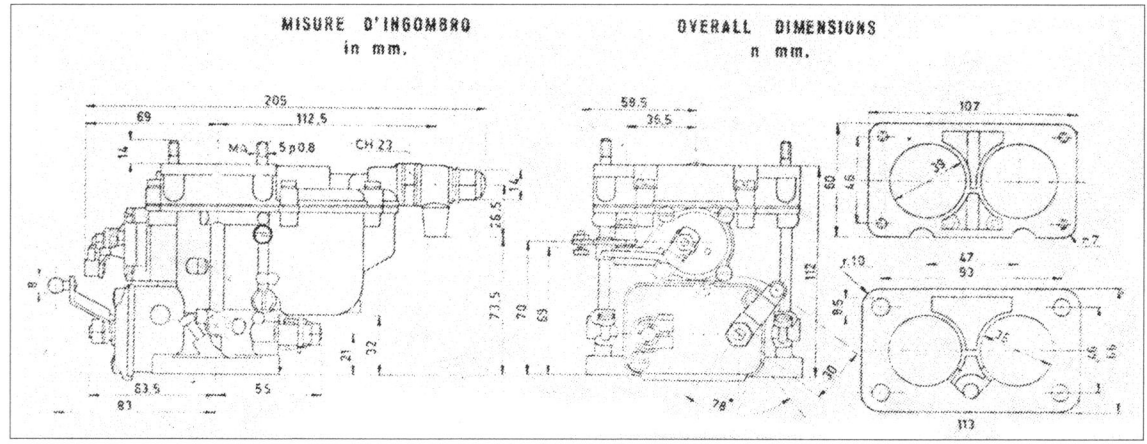

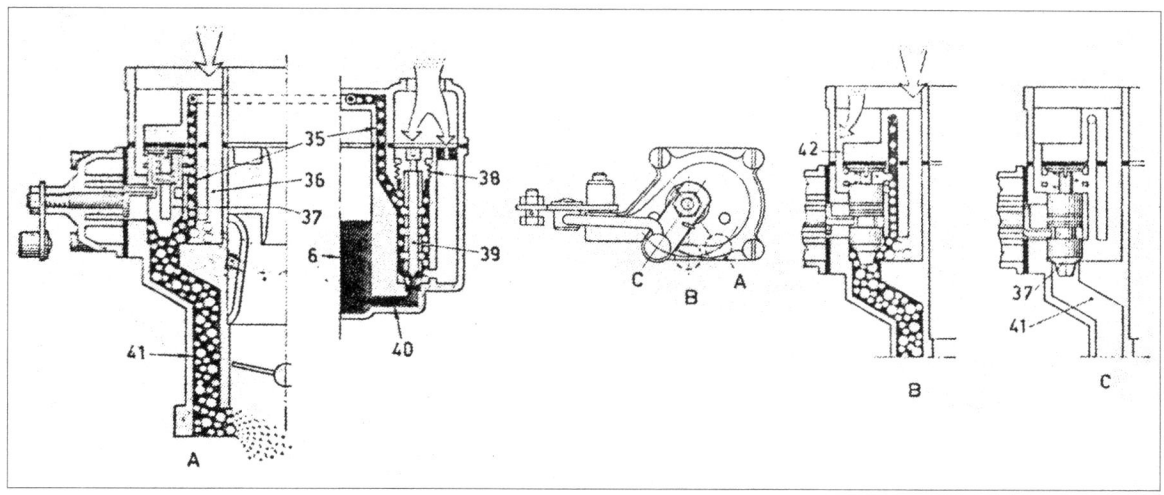

Figure 4

STARTING DEVICE - Fig. 4
The fuel passes from the bowl (6) to the starting device through duct (40) and the starting jet (39). Emulsioned with the air coming from the carburetor air intake (calibrated by the air corrector jet (38) it reaches the plunger chamber (37), through duct (35), where it is mixed with air from duct (36); this mixture is then aspirated through duct (41), so permitting ready starting of the engine. (Diagram A).

As soon as the engine is started, partially close the starter device (Diagram B).

In these conditions a further airflow, from duct (42) leans the mixture delivered by the starter, so permitting normal working with a cold engine.

As the engine warms up, however, this mixture is too rich and in excessive supply, so the starting device must be progressively cut out as the temperature of the engine rises.

With the starting device disconnected, this plunger (37) closes duct (41) stopping the call for mixture. (Digram C).

Instructions for use of starting device

In order to get the best results possible from the starting device, the most important instructions for use are summarised below:

Engine Starting
Starting from cold - Fully insert the starting device. Position "A" On starting reduce its degree of connection.

Starting with engine warm - Partial insertion of the starting device is all that is needed in this case. Position "B".

Putting the vehicle to work - During warming-up of the engine, even with the vehicle in motion, progressively disconnect the device with successive manipulations so as to have always a supplementary distribution of mixture, sufficient but no more than necessary for normal functioning of the engine. Position "B".

Normal running of the vehicle - As soon as the engine has reached a temperature sufficient for normal running, cut out the starting device. Position "C".

NOTES

NOTES

Lightning Source UK Ltd.
Milton Keynes UK
UKHW05f2301150618
324249UK00001BA/4/P